Jet Provost
The Little Plane with the Big History

Jet Provost
The Little Plane with the Big History

BOB CLARKE

AMBERLEY PUBLISHING

First published 2008

Amberley Publishing Plc
Cirencester Road, Chalford,
Stroud, Gloucestershire, GL6 8PE

www.amberley-books.com
British Library Cataloguing in Publication Data.
A catalogue record for this book is available from the British Library.

isbn 978 1 84868 097 5

Typesetting and Origination by Diagraf (www.diagraf.net)
Printed in Great Britain

For all the Leeming Lineys

Contents

Acknowledgements

As usual with a work like this, there is a long list of individuals who deserve thanks. I mention them in no specific order of importance. Mary Guy (College Librarian at the Royal Air Force College, Cranwell), Bryan Knight, Roy Davey, Bryan John Beames, Jim Duncan, John Cooper, Paddy Kinloch, Ed Austin, Mal Shaw, John Moran and George Dobie. The Australian Transport Safety Bureau, New Zealand Royal Air Force, Flt Lt John Letton and Lt Cmd 'Danny' Daniell. A special mention goes to Laurie Bean for his assistance and helpful conversation on all things Jet Provost. Also Dick Ansley, without whom the Strikemaster section would be much the poorer. Pete James and others, who managed to source a number of rare photographs; Mick Ryan who supplied some splendid insight and photos regarding the JP operations in the Far East. All those reporters from Flight International, Aircraft Illustrated, Air Pictorial, and others who have reported on the progress of the aircraft over the years, and in so doing created the primary record in some areas. Campbell McCutcheon, who rescued this book in its hour of need. Special thanks to Air Marshall Sir Dusty Miller KBE for agreeing to write the forward to the book. Finally of course my family. Luckily they like airshows!

Quotations of Hansard and other Government sources come through Parliamentary Licence No. P20080000286 28/09/2008 – 27/09/2013.

As in many illustrated works of this kind, a number of photographs are unaccredited. This is not for want of trying to locate the copyright owners. So, if you believe one of yours appears, please let me know so I can rectify the situation.

I hope I have mentioned everybody concerned; however, as always, the blame for any mistakes rests with me and me alone.

Foreword

I was delighted to be invited to write a forward to Bob Clarke's 'Jet Provost - The Little Plane with the Big History' for a number of reasons. First, I agree wholeheartedly with his opening sentiment that the Jet Provost was, until now, the unsung hero of several chapters of British defence history: it provided the bedrock of training for several generations of Royal Air Force pilots over the better part of 4 decades. Second, the story is a wonderful illustration of British ingenuity and entrepreneurial acumen in anticipating a requirement ahead of time, and then selling it most successfully at home and overseas, most notably at a time of a dramatically contracting British aircraft industry. Finally, the Jet Provost formed a crucial part in my own development from an ex-Halton Brat to a successful frontline pilot, both as student and a short while later as a flying instructor.

Even acknowledging the striking reductions in the Royal Air Force in the late-1940s and early-1950s, it is easy to overlook the size of the frontline of the 1960s, 1970s and 1980s, and in doing so fail to appreciate the scale of the training task to keep operational conversion units supplied with young pilots prepared to the required standard. Throughout this period the performance and complexity of the frontline aircraft types, especially in the fast-jet community, developed at a rapid pace, yet many continued to possess handling characteristics that demanded top quality motor skills and coordination from their pilots. Here, the Jet Provost provided a low cost and extremely reliable and robust platform for the *ab initio* pilots to learn the fundamentals of their trade. The overriding majority of pilots who contributed to the successful conclusion of the Cold War were products of that era of training, as were those who fought and won the hot war in the South Atlantic in 1982, and again the first Gulf War in 1991 and operations in the Balkans in the mid-1990s. I should add, for fear of retribution if I did not, that the Jet Provost also made an invaluable contribution to the entire range of airborne training other than just pilots, all of which Bob Clarke covers with admirable completeness in his book.

Having had the opportunity to read the manuscript, I was particularly taken by Bob's description of the genesis of the Jet Provost and its subsequent development up to and including the final build standard of its many variants. It truly encapsulates the confidence of a few far-seeing men who invested company money in a private venture development against what was at the time an unendorsed requirement. Clearly the turmoil in the aerospace industry in the post-war period, succinctly captured in the early chapters of this book, was a motivator in itself, but the risks were staggering. I also enjoyed the image of the early prototypes being hand made (the phrase lash up comes to mind), often from the materials and parts available on the bench at the time, and the subsequent maintenance nightmares once the aircraft were in service. I suspect the Jet Provost was probably not the first aircraft to be built in this manner and from my own experience was certainly not the last. Nevertheless, it is of enormous credit to the Royal Air Force tradesmen and an endorsement of their training and professionalism that they take such matters in their stride, invariably accompanied by razor sharp wit.

With over 1200hrs of Jet Provost time in my log book, the aircraft has secured a place in my heart and is the subject of many late night anecdotes that will never be committed to print – well, not before the 100-year clause has elapsed at least. I have not counted how many students went on to build successful flying careers having passed through my hands, although I am convinced that most did so despite my best efforts as an instructor at 3 FTS, RAF Leeming. I happened to be instrumental in the untimely destruction of XW331 for which I received a monumental clip round the ear from AOC 23 Group, but happily Bob Clarke's trawl through the accident reports does not go back that far so saves my embarrassment. During that time I had the immense privilege of flying as No 2 to Bob Thompson's Lead in the 1973 Gemini display team. Other than the signature Mirror formation mentioned by the author, our display comprised (very) close formation aerobatics, synchronised individual aerobatics, and lots of rejoins – here the Viper's modest ability to convert fuel into thrust often had me not quite getting back into formation in time, to the point where the Leader threatened to break my left arm and set it in plaster at full reach in order that I would never be able to retard the throttle from full power. I took that as encouragement! I also strongly support the comment in the book from the Poachers in 1975 relating to the rather heavy flying controls, but sometimes pulling hard was easy if you had the right incentive. The aerial visibility in Germany throughout the Summer of 1973 was notoriously poor although it only had an effect on our display at Krefeld on 19 August. Having launched out of Köln/Bonn in the early afternoon, Bob Thompson groped his way through the industrial heartland of Germany towards the display site in bright sunshine but with in-flight visibility that was right on the limits (code for downright ghastly). Having found our holding point and heard on the radio that the Red Arrows had missed the display site altogether, Bob decided to take a look for himself but cautioned me to remain in line astern formation as we may never find each other again if we separated. One brief flypast confirmed that none of the show sequences we had rehearsed were going to be suitable but, on the request of the controller on the ground, Bob decided that we could complete a couple of flypasts in close formation before returning to Koln/Bonn. All was going well, albeit from the inside of a very murky goldfish bowl, until Bob further decided that we should do formation barrel roll before departure. From the back of the formation I was aware that we were pulling up and rolling, but I soon became conscious that we had not pulled up very far. As we came over the top of the barrel roll the windscreen rapidly filled with bright green grass and the most enormous windmill I had ever seen in my life. As the g hastily increased the windmill disappeared close under the nose of my aircraft and my gallant Leader's voice was to be heard on the radio: "Are you still there No 2?"

Bob Clarke is to be congratulated for assembling the mass of factual, technical and historical detail in this book and then presenting it in the context of changing British defence policy, alongside a number of anecdotes that give a genuine feel for life operating the Jet Provost from the positions of both aircrew and groundcrew. It is truly a great book about 'The Little Plane with the Big History'. I hope you enjoy it as much as I have.

Air Marshal Sir Dusty Miller KBE

Preface

On 27 July 1981 I arrived at the guardhouse at RAF Leeming, unimpressed. Having spent six weeks' basic training in the freezing cold of a Lincolnshire winter at RAF Swinderby, and a further four months of mechanic training at the equally inhospitable Halton, I reckoned the RAF owed me a decent posting. I remember the jubilation of those going to Vulcan, Phantom and Jaguar squadrons, while a couple of us made light of the fact we had been posted to Jet Provost training units. For a few weeks after arriving I thought joining the RAF had been one big mistake.

A constant round of SWO's working party, I became quite an expert with barbed-wire traps and sandbags, and that feeling of isolation one gets when in a new environment didn't help. The station had been built as part of the northern expansion of bomber bases, just prior to the outbreak of war. By 1942 it had become the home of 63 Base, Royal Canadian Air Force. Recently I discovered there had been a small-scale revolt by the RCAF servicemen due to the poor conditions, so I hadn't been the only miserable one at the station! Afterwards Leeming had been home to such aircraft as the Meteor and Gloster Javelin, before becoming (like so many other stations in the North East) a flight-training base, populated predominantly by the Jet Provost.

The first visit to my new section was a real eye-opener. I had worked with the JP, in training, as something to take apart and marshal around on the airfield at Halton. I was also used to them in the air, as my family lived smack in the middle of the No. 11 low flying zone, much to my father's annoyance – he worked nights for a local firm. But I was not used to twenty-two of them at once! Intermingled with, on occasion, Phantoms, Hunters, Bulldogs, Hercules, F-111s, Starfighters, Doves, Devons and Chinooks – the list was endless. This was an exciting place. Even John Paul II and Jan Leeming visited the station, although not for the same reason I suspect.

It wasn't long before I was one of the 'Leeming Lineys', spending some extremely memorable nights at The Fleece in Northallerton and Buzby Stoop. Unfortunately, it did not last. I was posted to Lyneham in February 1983, and so spent just eighteen months on the Jet Provost. I did not miss them. True, I had spent a few hours in the spare seat, and on a number of occasions actually buzzed my sleeping dad, but now was the time for bigger things. Lyneham opened up my world, quite literally, with trips to Germany, trips to Ascension Island and trips to Wootton Bassett where I met my wife. Jet Provosts were something to be kept quiet during those long sessions in the pub. Or so I thought. It turned out quite a number of my colleagues had actually wanted to spend time with the JP. Working on frontline stations had bee,n throughout the 1980s, a gruelling cavalcade of exercises, detachments and gateguard, and it was well known that very little of that went on at Flight Training Schools. By the time I reached St Athan, which it has to be said was the worst station in the RAF in the 1980s, the 'red and white peril' had ceased to be a dark secret, becoming more an object of affection.

The aircraft outlived my RAF career. By 1990 St Athan had finally finished me off, and I left – one of the best moves I ever made, it has to be said. The JP was eventually replaced by the Tucano. Press releases at the time proclaimed, 'The Shorts Tucano is replacing the Jet Provost as the RAF's basic trainer. The Shorts Tucano climbs faster and has twice the range and endurance of the Jet Provost, yet uses only half the fuel and a third of the maintenance manpower.' Having serviced a few Tucanos at Boscombe Down, all I can say is that the PR chap must have got the aircraft mixed up.

Now of course the aircraft is a museum piece. It is predominately seen flying at airshows, and I am proud to point out the different marks to my less-than-enthusiastic children (It's a sad fact that as girls get older they become less impressed by the colour of an aircraft and more interested in the driver). Now I lecture in aircraft engineering to apprentices at Boscombe Down, and never miss an opportunity to regale them with tales of the 'mighty Jet Provost'. So what is the reason for this book? Well, I do not believe this unsung Cold War warrior should be allowed to go quietly. A book search on practically any other aircraft type brings forward a bewildering number of publications. With the iconic status of aircraft like the Lightning, Vulcan, Hunter, or indeed any second-rate American machine the list is endless. But what of the Jet Provost? Every pilot in the RAF trained on the type between the mid-1950s and the early 1990s. Its versatile qualities ensured that trainee pilots got the very best grounding in their pursuit of excellence. It was indeed the bedrock on which all pilot training stood throughout the Cold War.

As is so often the case, researching a project throws up new information (for the author at least), and this has certainly been the case here. While I was stationed at Lyneham, a small silver aircraft known as a 'Piston Provost' was hangared there. On occasion we would wander over and have a look. Its proportions were slightly familiar, especially the empennage. It should have been: the Percival Provost as it was more correctly called was the forerunner to the good old JP. Some twenty years later, I have come to realise that this aircraft too was a major contributor to pilot training in the post-war period, and a best-seller as well. So it is impossible to recount the story of the Jet Provost without more than a passing mention of its piston-powered predecessor. Or indeed the company that was responsible for both. And what of exports? Well, you will be interested to hear that both the Piston (I will use that term throughout this text to differentiate) and Jet Provost export derivatives saw action in a number of countries around the world.

The information for this work has not come easily. Luckily I have spent a lot of the past fifteen years discussing prehistoric sites through my work with the University of Bath. Consequently I am used to knitting tentative evidence into something workable. Little did I know how useful working with sites 4,000 years old would be when it came to the JP. It turns out that one of the reasons for the lack of publications is the fact that no company archive appears to have survived. When the manufacturing site at Luton was disposed of, after the merger into the British Aircraft Corporation in the early 1960s, the entire archive went in the skip. All that remains concerning Provost development are those papers produced by the various establishments where the aircraft was tested. Ministry and Treasury papers survive in the National Archive and a few other gems are in private collections, however tracking these down has been like trying to locate the blueprints for Stonehenge. Naturally, Hendon holds plenty of information about the service history of the type. But the fact remains that we have lost a great deal, and, when you consider Percival's contribution to British aviation, the loss is so much the greater. It doesn't stop there: the records of Airwork also appear to have gone the same way, removing information of the Strikemasters that served in Oman and the Middle East, not that any of this has deterred me.

It would be tempting to follow the majority of aircraft publications and infuse the book with pictures, padded out with a few statistics. However that neither informs the reader nor allows the character of the aircraft to be described. This aircraft, with a forty-year history (mostly at the hands of students), has seen more than its fair share of scrapes, and it would be amiss if we didn't explore these, at least. Consequently, this project centres as much around the human elements of the Jet Provost as it does on the technical. I hope that by interspersing all the other information chronicled here with accounts from those who built, maintained and flew the JP, the aircraft's full character will be revealed. Selfishly I hope this will allow the reader to experience the aircraft as I did then, worryingly over twenty-five years ago. So strap yourself in as I recount the story of the Jet Provost: The Little Plane with the Big History.

1.
Pilots, Percival and the Provost

It would be impossible to relay the story of the Jet Provost without first presenting a brief account of flying training in Britain, especially since the aircraft is inextricably linked with aircrew training. It is also important to understand where the Jet Provost comes from, and it may surprise the reader to learn that it has a direct lineage with a training aircraft first proposed in 1944. This first chapter covers the journey, from the inception of coherent flying training, through to the final production aircraft of the Percival Provost some fifty years later.

'IN THAT DECORUM – PERFECTLY INSTRUCTED'

Competent and relevant training is the fundamental to any air force. Consequently, the concept of adequately trained individuals has been around almost as long as that of aircraft themselves. Indeed, the earliest training establishment in the world, Central Flying School (CFS) originally located at Upavon, proves the point. By the outbreak of World War I the development of aerial tactics as a component of warfare was only just gaining recognition. Prior to that, aircraft had been relegated to spotting for artillery, reconnaissance and naval duties.

By the Battle of the Somme, in July 1916, the Royal Flying Corps could boast thirty-one operational squadrons stationed in France. Casualties from July to mid November (308 airmen) brought demands for an increase of squadrons to fifty-six and for a further twenty by the end of 1916. The immediate answer was to open further flying schools in Britain, and form twenty reserve squadrons in Canada. Before the Somme, training had been a complicated affair. Pilots attended an 'Elementary' Training School (TS), then took their Flying Certificate test, examined by the Royal Aero Club, and on gaining their 'ticket' were posted onto higher or advanced Training Schools for specialist instruction. It was not until training losses became so bad they were affecting morale that flying training was finally made safer, by the introduction of a specifically designed course.

With the direction of Robert Smith-Barry, flying training was revolutionised. Some elements of this syllabus are still taught today. Firstly, the student position was switched from rear to front seat, giving a far more representative view. Extensive classroom lectures covered the characteristics of flight, how to control a multitude of airframe types and what the aircrafts limits were, before taking practical instruction. Pilots were also shown what to do if a dangerous situation arose. Prior to this, recovering from a spin or stall was more often through luck than judgment. Key to this new flying training regime was the Qualified Flying Instructor, preferably with lots of hours' flying and genuine combat experience. In July 1917 the School of Special Flying was formed at Gosport, with the sole intention of instructing a new breed of QFI, one that worked to a syllabus rather than 'flew by the seat of his pants.'

Meanwhile, training stations were springing up across the country, capitalising on local volunteers eager to fly. However the situation was far from adequate: the level of training was totally dependent on the ability of the Training Brigade instructors that ran them. In an attempt to standardise the situation a new type of aerodrome, the Training Depot Station, was devised. More than sixty were in existence by the end of the war. Unfortunately most were utilised as demobilisation centres, as they were often still under construction at the time of the Armistice. After the war flying training was trimmed to the bone. Just a few stations survived the swinging cuts successive Governments forced on the newly formed RAF, which came into being on 1 April 1918.

In the course of the 1930s, it became increasingly clear that the pursuit of peace with regard to Europe was a flawed policy. From 1935 the Royal Air Force began an ambitious process of expansion, primarily in an attempt to keep pace with German and Italian rearmament. Naturally competent pilots were a major component of any increase, and by 1936 training units had been formed around the country. By 1939 fourteen Flying Training Schools (FTS) existed in Britain, including Hullavington, South Cerney, Ternhill and Shawbury; all were also home to Aircraft Storage Units (ASU). These were supported by a number of Relief Landing Grounds by 1940. Throughout the 1930s a number of Auxiliary Squadrons had helped to plug the pilot gap, and this was supplemented by University Air Squadrons. However, these organisations were quickly absorbed into the mainstream aircrew programme at the outbreak of war.

Once a student had been selected, he could look forward to a period of basic flying instruction at one of the many Elementary Flying Training Schools (EFTS) around Britain. EFTS were privately run ventures, most under contract since 1934. By the end of 1941, twenty-nine such 'contract airfields' were training aircrew. However EFTS in Britain were just the tip of the iceberg. The Air Ministry instigated a massive training program with the help of Dominion Governments. Known in Britain as the Empire Air Training Scheme, the Government proposed the idea in September 1939, that fifty EFTS would eventually be established in locations as far away as Australia, Canada and New Zealand. A student would undertake a basic course on the Tiger Moth, before progressing on to the North American Harvard. Graduates of these schools would then receive advanced training in Canada, before proceeding to Britain for service with the RAF. Once back in the country they were posted to training aerodromes such as Hullavington, for familiarization training in map reading, blackout and weather conditions. Specialist training was administered at Operational Conversion Units. Bomber Command used Heavy Conversion Units, often located at an existing squadron airfield. To compliment this they also operated the Lancaster Finishing School, with units at Lindholme, Faldingworth, Hemswell, Feltwell, Syerston and Ossington.

COLD WAR

At the end of World War II, the RAF faced some stark realities. Naturally, the force needed to be reduced in size: by May 1945 the airfleet numbered 55,469 aircraft, whilst the personnel strength was 1,079,835, nearly 200,000 of which were aircrew.

The problem now was how to reduce this number whilst keeping an effective and credible level of defence. In 1947 the Air Staff proposed 'Plan E'. The RAF was to be trimmed to 1,500 aircraft, spread across fifty-one fighter squadrons, forty-one bomber squadrons, thirteen maritime aircraft squadrons and forty-two transport squadrons. A further twelve reserve squadrons would also be formed. The Cabinet thought otherwise, and by 1948 the numbers had been reduced to half that suggested by the Air Staff. Manpower attrition was little different, by 1948 the Royal Air Forces' personnel strength was down to 325,000 and in considerable crisis. It had not been possible to dictate who was demobbed when, consequently aircrew and ground crew with specialist knowledge on new equipment, especially jet-powered aircraft and missile technology, were lost.

The RAF trade structure was also in dire need of modernisation. Throughout the war trade groups had numbered just over one hundred, with all the administrative headaches that accompanied them. By 1950 this had been reduced to a far more manageable twenty-two. Unfortunately the same could not be said for the General Duties Branch (flying). Throughout the war aircrew were a mixture of commissioned and non-commissioned, demarcated by rank alone. In July 1946 an attempt to further differentiate between the two groups led to the creation of such titles as Pilot One and Navigator Two. Complimenting this, a new series of Aircrew Messes were introduced, further removing aircrew from ground crew. By 1950 the whole scheme was abandoned as practically unworkable.

Central Flying School

The Central Flying School (CFS) was re-formed at Little Rissington, Gloucestershire, in May 1946, and continues today to be the foundation of all modern Tri-Service Flying Training. CFS courses originally contained specialist elements, such as the instrument rating system for Transport Command. However, by 1948 a new scheme had been devised for the training of pilots, and that year CFS was tasked with turning out 240 Qualified Flying Instructors (QFIs). The range of aircraft utilised throughout the QFI training course was, as one would imagine, comprehensive. The Tiger Moth, Harvard, Mosquito, Lancaster, Spitfire were all available. Courses also included one hour on the de Havilland Vampire to give some jet experience. Basic flight training was also restructured to cover the rapidly changing requirements of the post-war RAF. Of major importance was the streamlining of flying training itself. From 1949 the student would have one instructor, from basics through to his wings.

The Air Ministry also began the process of upgrading their training aircraft, especially the Tiger Moths, a venerable veteran from the early 1930s. The RAF originally ordered thirty-five dual-control Moth Is, designated the DH 60T, in the late 1920s. A further order increased the number with fifty DH 82A Tiger Moth IIs powered by the more powerful de Havilland Gipsy Major I engine. The aircraft entered service with Central Flying School in February 1932, and by the start of World War II the RAF had 500 of the aircraft. Naturally this rapidly increased. The production run in Britain alone was over 7,000 with a large number built by shadow factories. The aircraft was the last of the RAF biplane trainers, equipping an incredible eighty-three FTS by the end of the war. Whilst the airframe was very forgiving (a definite bonus for a primary training aircraft), the type was far too basic for post-war pilot exercises. Consequently those retained on charge were downgraded to University Air Squadrons (UAS). When a replacement was sought for the UAS, de Havilland came up with the answer – the DHC Chipmunk

Tiger Moth. The trusty de Havilland Tiger Moth was produced in large numbers throughout WWII. Over 7,000 were built; however, post-war flying training demanded a 'modern' platform.

The Chipmunk was a radical detachment from previous basic trainer designs. The construction comprised an all-metal, low wing, tandem, single-engine airplane sporting a conventional tail wheel. It had fabric-covered control surfaces and wing aft of the spar to reduce weight. CF-DIO-X, the Chipmunk prototype, flew for the first time on 22 May 1946 at Downsview, Toronto. Designed by Wsiewołod Jakimiuk, a Polish engineer employed at the company's Canadian plant, it was the first purely Canadian design. Two aircraft were shipped to the United Kingdom and were placed on evaluation at A&AEE Boscombe Down. Subsequently the Chipmunk was ordered as a basic trainer for the Royal Air Force, against specification 8/48. De Havilland built 735 Chipmunks at their UK plants. The first operational RAF aircraft were flown by the Oxford UAS from February 1950; thereafter, the type replaced the Tiger Moth with all seventeen UAS. The type went on to equip many RAF Volunteer Reserve flying schools in the early 1950s as well.

PERCIVAL, PROCTOR AND THE PRENTICE

The Chipmunk, however, was just the beginning of the modernisation programme, and by mid-1948 the Air Ministry was taking delivery of its new trainer – the Percival Prentice. The Prentice, built to specification T.23/43, was intended to revolutionise basic training, operating in the *ab initio* (from first principles) role. During the war the Tiger Moth had relatively easy to handle during the initial phase, ensuring all but the very worst pilots made it through to the next stage. From there, if the student failed the transition, they were re-mustered to other flying duties such as navigator or bomb aimer. The T.23/43 dictated a more complex training aircraft, mirroring at least some of the attributes of its frontline counterparts. This was intended to expose any shortfall demonstrated by the student pilot more quickly, meaning they could be easily weeded out at an earlier stage. Naturally, the savings of operating cost in and reduced airframe hours were a major focus. The specification stipulated that the aircraft should be able to operate in all weathers, carry full radio equipment, and be fully aerobatic. As a further cost-cutting initiative, it was to carry a third seat for passenger to gain air experience. Proposals put forward by Percival Aircraft were accepted in late 1944, starting a chain of events that was to end with the Jet Provost.

The Prentice was not the first military contract Percival had won. In 1938 they had submitted plans in response to Air Ministry Specification 20/38, for a radio trainer and communications aircraft – the Proctor. The prototype first flew on 8 October 1939, and the aircraft was subsequently placed in production for both the RAF and Royal Navy. The Proctor was a development of the Percival Vega Gull, the company's major pre-war success story. In 1933, after a period of self-building the highly successful touring aircraft 'The Gull', Percival Aircraft Company was floated on the stock exchange. By 1934 aircraft were being produced at a factory established at Gravesend, and by 1938 the company was the first occupant of the newly constructed Luton Airport, a site they were to dominate for the next 40 years. By the mid-1930s the Air Ministry was re-equipping its training fleet. The Percival Proctor was utilised throughout the war, with over a thousand eventually being built. Unfortunately, the story of the Percival Prentice was not to be so distinguished.

Early test fights demonstrated that the Prentice was extremely unpredictable. Modifications were needed to stop the aircraft flipping over during gentle turns. The

Percival Prentice. The first aircraft for the service arrived at RAF Hullavington on 27 August 1947. Four hundred were eventually delivered; unfortunately the type was not well received. (Photograph by Adrian Pingstone)

flap area had little clearance with the ground and a less-than-gentle landing could cause major structural damage, but it was in the spin that the aircraft was most dangerous. After two to three turns, the spin would flatten out. Recovery after this was almost impossible without the aid of an anti-spin parachute. It was not a good start for a training aircraft. The first production Prentice aircraft for service arrived at RAF Hullavington on 27 August 1947 to undergo evaluation trails, and by July the following year the first squadron deployment was underway for CFS, at RAF South Cerney. The RAF finally received 400 Prentices, 75 of which were constructed under licence by Blackburn Aircraft Ltd. Interestingly, as the new aircraft were being welcomed into service, their days were already numbered. Through the earlier trials the Air Ministry had already recognised that the Prentice did not fit their requirements, and a new specification, T.16/48, was issued. Over thirty speculative designs were submitted for what was potentially a very lucrative contract, but they had little chance against a new Percival design, the P.56, later to become the Provost.

P.56 Provost

It was well known in aviation circles that the Air Ministry was disappointed with the Prentice and would, in the near future, be seeking a replacement. Percival had decided to build a possible replacement prototype designed by Arthur Bage as a private venture, with the hope of getting a head start, and was well on the way to

Percival Provost. WE522 first flew on 23 February 1950 and with little extra work the aircraft almost totally satisfied the Air Ministry's requirements. A testament to private venture planning. (Percival Aircraft)

completion by the time the specification was issued. The initial prototype aircraft was powered by an Armstrong Siddeley Cheetah 17 radial engine. WE522 first flew on 23 February 1950, and with little extra work the aircraft almost totally satisfied the Air Ministry's requirements. However, this was nearly not the case. Bryan Knight was the Senior Weight Analyst for Percival at the time, and later described the Provost's first tentative steps:

"Provost P.56 prototype first test flight . . . with half the factory out there on the field at Luton to watch this exciting day in Percivals' history! Full throttle applied . . . speed builds up as it trundles across the grass . . . then leaps wildly into the air in a fashion reminiscent of a modern jet fighter applying full afterburner on the deck!

"A few moments later, a white-faced Dick Wheldon, our Chief Test Pilot, emerges from the cockpit after wrestling the bird back to earth!"

"Now which of you bods couldn't read his slide rule correctly?"

"A slip of a decimal place, somewhere along the line during design calculations, had resulted in the main forging that held the new-fangled all-flying tail being "off and up" by about 7 degrees. The result . . . it took much throttle manipulation and full-down "elevator" just to maintain level flight. At a subsequent post-mortem conference, "someone" suggested, as a joke, the interim fix of sawing through the aft fuselage, bending it down and re-riveting it back together with a big splice plate. The Model Shop took this as gospel and proceeded to do so! That old gal flew all over the world for many years as a marketing plane, with that drooping rear end, and may still be flying for all I know!"

Once corrected, the handling qualities were far removed from that of the Prentice. It was easy to fly, but as responsive as the fighter in some areas. Both the Provost and its only constructed competitor, the Handley-Page HPR.2, appeared at Farnborough that same year, but by then Percival were on the home straight. After re-evaluating the aircraft, this time powered by the far superior supercharged Alvis Leonides 25 radial engine and with a three-bladed propeller, a maximum speed of 200mph was achieved. The supercharging meant that the aircraft could climb to 23,000ft far quicker than the Cheetah-engined prototype, allowing for more instructional duration at a safer height. The engine was air-cooled, ram air passing through the circular duct surrounding the propeller hub and then out through two ducts either side of the fuselage. This in itself caused a few problems, as if the duct was deformed in any way it set up an asymmetric airflow down the side of the fuselage and over the tailplane. This, coupled with the prop-wash, tended to cause some interesting pitching and rolling; strengthening rectified this. There was one other engine-related vice that only came to light when taking off. The Leonides 25 radial engine produced a phenomenal amount of torque and as the wheels came off could, if the pilot was not paying attention, drag the aircraft sideways.

Construction

The aircraft was an all-metal semi-monocoque construction. The cockpit was side-by-side seating arranged over the lateral axis, a rear-sliding canopy, which could be jettisoned in an emergency, and backlight panels for extra visibility. The windscreen comprised eight separate transparencies, five of toughened glass, and three across the top Perspex. The complex windscreen arrangement was stressed as part of the support structure of the engine housing and fire bulkhead, forward of the cockpit. The rear fuselage was constructed around four longerons, giving the appearance of an almost square section, housing the radio equipment and battery. The empennage comprised a typical arrangement – horizontal tailplane and elevators, single vertical stabiliser and rudder, all horn balanced. The wings contained two fireproof fuel tanks, which fed the

Percival Provost. WE530 supplied as the Air Ministry demonstrator. The supercharged Alvis Leonides 25 radial engine allowed a top speed of 200mph and height of 23,000ft.

engine via a collector tank under the cockpit floor, supplied by an electric pump to the injectors at start-up and thereafter by Engine Driven Pump (EDP).

The undercarriage was distinctive: to give clearance to the propeller whilst the aircraft was taking off, a long-stroke shock absorber was used for both main undercarriages. However, on this aircraft there was no immediate problem getting onto the wing and into the aircraft, as it was supported by a tail wheel, allowing personnel to step up onto the trailing edge. The aircraft was fitted, where possible, with access panels, making servicing and repair that much quicker and easier, a definite bonus with training aircraft. The September edition of *Flight* went as far as to say 'There seems no doubt, in fact, that RAF Training Command will receive in their new basic trainers an aircraft most likely among all others to date to find favour with instructors, pupils and ground crews alike.'

Into Service

An initial order for 200 aircraft was placed in May 1951, the first aircraft being delivered to Central Flying Schools' Basic Training Squadron at RAF South Cerney in 1953. CFS QFIs set about devising the flying programme and syllabus for the new aircraft. The first aircraft arrived at No.6 FTS Ternhill in October 1953, and other stations, including Hullavington, Worksop and Feltwell received new airframes quickly after that. By the late 1950s the Provost could be encountered at many RAF Flying Training establishments. Nearly 400 aircraft were to eventually see service with the RAF, some, however, were destined to train Royal Navy pilots. No 1 FTS, reopened at Syerston in 1955, was tasked with providing initial training for members

Percival Provost. WV475, originally of No.1 FTS, Syerston in 1955, was tasked with FAA flying training.

of the Royal Navy using the Provost. By September 1957 the school had moved again, this time to the station it still occupys – RAF Linton-on-Ouse.

Of course, it is only when an aircraft has been in service for a while and started to accrue some flying hours that the true nature of the beast is revealed. Top of the list of surprises was the serviceability of the powerful engine. Notwithstanding the effect of torque on the aircrafts direction at take-off, as Cpl Bryan John Beames RAF apprentice remembers:

'In use at South Cerney we had several 'fatals' with them, primarily because of engine failure. If my memory serves me correctly the cylinder heads used to crack quite frequently and were then modified at Alvis's. After that, and while still rated at 550hp at plus 8 boost, the pistons started to collapse, so in the end the Leonides was downrated to plus 4 boost after which we had no more problems – not with engine failures anyway.'

Interestingly, this affected the handling of the aircraft, as flying instructor Flt Lt Roy Davey remembers:

"The Piston Provost had an Alvis Leonides engine, but because of – I suspect – reliability problems, its maximum power available had been down rated."

As with all aircraft systems, especially the engine, once servicing or the replacement of components had been completed, the power unit was required to have an 'engine ground run' to ensure its serviceability. Even this relatively straightforward task could present problems as Cpl Beames discovered at South Cerney.

"From hard experience we also learned that, on ground running an engine, it was always essential to have at least one side cowling attached. If you ran an engine without, the only things that secured the bottom panel (which formed the surround for the oil cooler) were two spring-loaded clips which would often ' let go ', allowing the panel to drop into the slipstream and then break away. We also found that, such was the slipstream over the tail surfaces during a run to max power, that no amount of tying the stick back was sufficient to keep the tail down – we had to have one or two guys lying on the tailplane as well. As usual we found this out the hard way, after what sounded like a very quick mag drop turned out to be a Provost that had lifted its tail far enough for the prop to dig quite a deep hole in the tarmac!"

Naturally not everything could be pinned down to a mechanical problem, on occasion an outside agency could be just as dangerous, as Jim Duncan, airframe fitter at Syerston in the late 1950s, remembers:

"My only memory of a Piston Provost was at Syerston in 1959. I was normally on the JP3 line, but had been given the task of fiddling with the rudder bar of the piston job. I was in an almost upside down, head near floor level, position, when the stick suddenly started whacking me! It took some time to wriggle my way free of the cockpit, before I noticed a pack of Air Cadets standing at the tail, with a mini-sergeant moving the elevator up and down while explaining its purpose in life to the teenie techs. His face went white as a sheet as I tore seven shades of shit out of him, and taught him words he wouldn't have heard outside a dockers' pub. I thought he was going to burst into tears, as he marched his wee pack off. The little sod reported me, and I received a Mk3 bollocking from some Sqn Ldr or other!"

Other incidences, as Cpl Beames remembers, were thankfully destined to remain a mystery!

"I was given the job of changing the centre tank on a Provost (piston variety). The a/c was just outside the hangar doors. The Provost fuel system was quite basic, and consisted of a tank on each side of the mainplane, which fed into a centre tank directly under the middle of the a/c. This then fed the engine via a small pressure pump (I think).There was a drop-down panel under the centre, which was secured by four king clamps. I had changed the tank, the two isolating valves having been turned off to start with. All that remained to be done was to turn on and wirelock the isolating valves. I had done one, when an a/c was pushed past me on the way to the compass base, for a swing after minor servicing. "Come and help push" yelled the Senior NCO in charge. "I'm just wrapping up Sarge, won't be a minute." "Do that when you get back," he said, "you'll only be gone five minutes". That five minutes became the best part of an hour and when I finally got back my a/c was nowhere to be seen. I was told the panel had been put back on and the a/c had gone on air test. At 4.45pm we were all waiting for the last a/c to land before going for tea. We saw it overhead at about 2,000 feet and, with a puff of black smoke from the exhaust the fan stopped. The last we saw of it was as it glided away and we subsequently learned that it had landed at Aston Down, a few miles away in a straight line! There, the centre panel must have been dropped, and the one remaining isolating valve turned on and wire locked. That's all I can imagine happened, and the following week the a/c was subjected to fuel flow tests etc. and much head scratching took place as the high-ups tried to discover what went wrong. It is still a mystery so far as I know, but I learned <u>never</u> to interrupt a job throughout my subsequent career."

Whilst in service, the aircraft continued to undergo trials. For a number of years the results obtained from models in wind tunnels had been in question, the aircraft often performing better than the model suggested. Subsequently in the mid 1950s the Royal Aircraft Establishment set about testing full size aircraft to compliment earlier results.

'The inverted spin and recovery characteristics were also investigated and are of special interest as these tests are probably the first recorded results in the inverted spin in this country.'

Full Scale Spinning Tests on the Percival Provost Mk.1
Tech Note Aero.2366. August 1955.

The results demonstrated that the aircraft recovered rapidly from the correct control movement in the inverted. It also revealed that the negative g effects during the spin made it difficult to keep the control column against the forward stops, unless one had a very long reach. Not holding the stick fully forward allowed the spin to speed up, increasing g effects. Also, a pilot in spin conditions experiences around -2.25 g at the head, however no effects are felt until the aircraft pulls out, then around 3 g may be experienced. The rapid fluctuation from one extreme to the other could cause momentary blackout and at low altitude this could prove fatal.

Conversion from one aircraft type to another showed up one peculiarity that is not encountered today. Flt Lt Roy Davey had been posted to CFS at RAF Little Rissington, on a flying instructor's course, as a Flying Officer:

"While I was at Little Rissington, on the course, in 1957, I almost tipped one onto its nose on my first solo, because I was used to tricycle under-carriage Hunters, which could not tip up, and the brakes on the PP were a bit fierce if you forgot to hold the stick right back."

Percival Provost. 461 aircraft were eventually delivered, seeing service across the world. (Bigbird Aviation)

And once in the air:

> "All piston-engined aircraft had a tendency to roll with the torque (i.e. in opposition to the rotational direction of the propeller), but the Piston Provost was quite marked. It was even more marked if you carried out an overshoot, close to the ground at low speed. The Tempest V had such a tendency that it would roll onto its back if you weren't careful (mind you, it had 3,000 horsepower available)."

Export

The Percival Provost also entered service with a number of foreign air forces, and in some cases paved the way for the Jet Provost and later Strikemasters. Tropical handling trials at Khartoum in May and June 1951 went some way to demonstrating that the aircraft was very capable in hot environments. Mainplane construction was such that a certain amount of under-wing stores could be carried, making it possible to operate an offensive capability. This was exploited in 1953, when a single demonstrator aircraft flew the Near East on a sales tour. The aircraft was ideal for close ground support. It had a rapid turn rate, making it extremely manoeuvrable, and could carry a mixture of weapons: two .303 machine guns with either a gun camera and two 250lb bombs, eight 25lb bombs and four 60lb rockets or six 60lb rockets. Armed versions were to see service with the Rhodesian Air Force (Mk.52), Burma, Iraq, Sudan and Muscat (Mk.53), whilst the Irish Air Corps took delivery of both trainers and the Mk.53.

The Burmese Air Force purchased 40 Mk.53 Provosts in two batches, to replace the Seafires and Spitfires in the ground-attack role. The Provost saw action with Government forces against rebel factions during the country's civil uprising. Used primarily to support the army, they proved difficult to use tactically if not in the hands of an extremely experienced pilot, especially over thick jungle. Despite this, the aircraft remained in service from 1958 to 1977. Those delivered to the Irish Air Corps became part of the pilot training framework. Students started out on the Chipmunk before progressing onto the Mk.51, a number of Mk.53s were acquired in the 1960s, and the aircraft only retired in 1977.

The Royal Rhodesian Air Force (RRAF) placed orders for the aircraft in 1953, and by November 1954 the first 4 T.51s had made the journey to Africa. The following year, twelve more aircraft had been delivered. Initially the aircraft were used as a basic trainer with 4 Sqd. RRAF, however by 1956 a number had been moved to 6 Sqd., performing internal security duties. By 1959 the Central Africa Federation, of which Rhodesia was a member, was experiencing major civil and political upheaval, and Provosts flew a number of operations in support of the Government Police. These ranged reconnaissance through to the airborne delivery of tear gas and propaganda leaflets. This came to a head in 1963, when the Central African Federation (CAF), of which Northern and Southern Rhodesia formed two thirds, finally collapsed.

At midnight on 22 October 1963 Northern Rhodesia gained her independence as Zambia, and by July 1964 Malawi was formed as an independent state from the third member of the CAF Nyasaland. Southern Rhodesia now demanded independence from British rule, however, this would only be possible through majority African rule, stated the recently elected Wilson Labour Government. After protracted discussion and recriminations, Dr Ian Smith declared the country independent on 11 November 1965, breaking his governments ties with Britain. Embargos ensued including, naturally, arms shipments. Interestingly when the CAF had dissolved, Rhodesia inherited the air force, but without spares the aircraft became increasingly difficult to operate. However, in the early 1970s the aircraft experienced a new lease of life, when a number of aircraft originally owned by Oman were acquired through secret negotiations. Over a period of eighteen months a slow trickle of British-registered Provosts appeared in the country, many refurbished before they arrived. The aircraft continued to be used in the reconnaissance role and was also used to track insurgents crossing the border until 1977.

Percival Provost. The Provost found success as a COIN aircraft with a number of air forces around the world.

Training Aid. A number of airframes found their way into training schools across the service. This one was stationed at RAF St. Athan. (Laurence Bean)

XF690, one of a number of aircraft still airworthy. (Pete James)

The Percival Provost was also used for air experience flight for members of the Air Training Corps. Flt Lt Roy Davey was collared for the job:

> "I flew the PP on the Flying Instructors Course in 1957. I went back on the headquarters staff in 1960. I only flew Piston Provosts between 30 April and 11 June 1961 as I was the PETLO (Pre-Entry Training Liaison Officer - one of those odd secondary duties officers had to do)- always on Sundays - and use to fly four or five cadets for fifteen minutes each, God, what a rush that must have been!"

Production of the aircraft for the Royal Air Force ceased in 195; however, the line continued at a reduced until the end of April 1960. The majority of the aircraft going to overseas contracts after 1956. The closure of the line was reported in *Flight International*:

> 'The handing over by Hunting Aircraft to the Irish Air Corps recently of the 461st and last Provost, the production line for this famous post-war trainer which originated as design study P.56 has come to an end. The prototype first flew on January 24, 1950, and following its adoption by the RAF the Provost has been ordered by the Air Forces of Rhodesia, Ireland, Burma, Iraq and the Sudan. In the RAF it is now being replaced by the Jet Provost under the new scheme of all-jet training, and at No 2 FTS at Syerston recently the last pupil to graduate on the Provost completed his training.'

Flight International 29 April 1960, p. 612.

As aircraft came to the end of their RAF life, a number were purchased back by the manufacturer and refurbished for foreign customers. Others made their way to Halton, St Athan and a number of other stations on ground instructional duties, preparing the next phase of engineers for service. Although it was only operated in its intended role for a relatively short space of time, the Piston Provost was a popular aircraft. It had good handling qualities. True, it had its quirks, but was consistent enough to allow the QFI to effectively judge his students' abilities. However, technological advances were now dictating that radial-piston engine aircraft were far detached from the rest of the training and frontline fleet. Even as the Provost was entering service, Hunting Percival were looking forward to the next generation of training aircraft. They had been at the front of the queue with the Provost, and intended to be in that advantageous and lucrative position again. On 26 June 1954, XD674, a design designated P.84, flew; all-through jet training moved a step closer, as did the iconic Jet Provost.

2.

Into the Jet Age

The move to 'all-through jet training' was inevitable; however, world events, as is so often the case, were to dictate the speed at which the Royal Air Force studied the proposition. On Sunday, 25 June 1950, North Korean forces breached the 38th Parallel, forcing the lightly armed Republic of Korea Army to retreat towards the South Korean capital, Seoul. That same day the United Nations Security Council met over the crisis.

> Noting with grave concern the armed attack on the Republic of Korea by forces from North Korea
>
> Determines that this action constitutes a breach of the peace; and
>
> Calls for the immediate cessation of hostilities;
>
> Calls upon the authorities in North Korea to withdraw forthwith their armed forces to the 38th parallel;

Security Council resolution 82 (1950) Resolution of 25 June 1950

By 27 June no such withdrawal or cessation of hostilities had been reported by UN officials, and the Republic of Korea was asking for international help.

> Recommends that the Members of the United Nations furnish such assistance to the Republic of Korea as may be necessary to repel the armed attack and to restore international peace and security in the area.

Security Council Resolution 83, 27 June 1950

The ensuing conflict sent shockwaves around the world. The West German Government saw the invasion as a ruse by Stalin to divert attention from the political problems in Central Europe. It was just possible that the East Germans could emulate the North Koreans and try to unify the country by force. The conflict became the first real test of the Truman Doctrine, especially as the Republic of Korea had specifically requested help through the United Nations. American aircraft were in action over the country from 27 June, and just a few days later troops were deployed from

33

neighbouring Japan. British units were committed on 28 August, the last were to leave in mid-1957.

Naturally, a major part of the conflict was the war in the air. It was during this phase that Western combat tactics underwent a radical revision, due to the introduction of the Mig-15. This aircraft was flown by North Korean and Soviet pilots from the outset, and was extremely successful against the majority of the UN forces' machines in the initial phase. Their opponents were a mixture of piston and first generation jet aircraft, the majority being outclassed by the more agile Migs. The RAF committed a number of support aircraft. It was the Fleet Air Arm, using predominantly the carrier-borne Sea Fury and Seafire that took the fight to the Communists. However it was the experiences of the RAAF that had the most effect on Whitehall.

At the beginning of the conflict No. 77 Squadron Royal Australian Air Force, stationed in Japan and equipped with F-51D Mustangs, began flying ground-support missions in support of UN forces. A number of contacts with MiG-15s 'encouraged' the squadron to re-equip with Meteor Mk8 fighters. Fifteen Mk8s and two Mk7s, two-seat training versions, were shipped to Japan in February 1951 to begin training, a further twenty Mk8s arrived during April 1951. The squadron flew its first Meteors on operational missions from 30 July 1951. Originally used as an escort fighter, the Meteor proved to be no match for the more agile MiG-15, and by December 1951 the squadron had been reduced to fourteen serviceable aircraft. Looking inwardly, British Air Defence, with its heavy reliance on Meteor and Vampire aircraft, appeared very out-gunned indeed.

Clearly, the Korean War had demonstrated a gap between British fighters and those it might well meet in the skies above Europe. To modernize the fighter fleet would mean the modernization of the training fleet as well. Unfortunately, the RAF was in the process of receiving its new trainer, yet another piston-driven aircraft, the P.56. Luckily, entrepreneurial skills had not yet been knocked out of the British aircraft manufacturers.

The introduction of the Mig-15 in Korea forced a radical rethink in flying training across the world.

P.84

If the P.56 Piston Provost proved anything, it was that the airframe had potential. Percival Aircraft had also demonstrated that speculative designs were still a viable proposition, especially if you could drive procurement policy. The prop-driven trainer was popular with both pilots and students, however the practice of training on airscrews and then converting to jets was rapidly becoming an outdated and expensive concept. Even as the P.56 was entering service with the RAF, the design team at Percival was busily planning a successor. And whilst all this was happening, the company's Service Liaison Officer, Wg Cdr Kingwell, was busy canvassing any senior officer that would listen to the concept of 'all-through jet training'.

The proposal was simple. Percival was convinced it could produce a basic airframe with low maintenance attributes, primarily with off-the-shelf components, but with considerably enhanced speed and height characteristics. Above all it would be jet powered, and thus be able to demonstrate a considerable saving in the initial training costs of the nation's military pilots. Those pilots would also receive valuable experience with high-speed aircraft earlier on in their training, making the conversion to operational aircraft a lot more effective.

Bryan Knight, working for the company at the time remembers:

"I was part of the Percival design team, and the whole idea behind the plane was that we could take an existing P.56 Provost and with a little juggling of the overall layout go almost "straight into production" ... at any rate the AM bought that idea!"

In March 1953 the Ministry of Supply, on behalf of the Air Ministry, placed a contract for £85,000 for the initial development work on the P.84. Under contract No. 9265, nine aircraft were subsequently delivered to the RAF for test and evaluation. By September Percival were in a position to announce some specifications and intentions; *Flight International* duly reported the points:

Percival Jet Provost

During March this year it was announced by the Under-Secretary of State for Air that the Air Ministry wished to consider the advisability of introducing a jet trainer into the R.A.F. at the basic stage, so that pupils could carry out the whole of their training on jet aircraft. Such a major change could not, he said, be decided on purely theoretical arguments, and the Government would make thorough practical trials within the training organization of the R.A.F. Later it was disclosed that an order had been placed with Percival Aircraft, Ltd., for a number of side-by-side two-seater jet trainers adapted from the Percival Provost T.l and depicted in model form at Farnborough last year. The Jet Provost differs from its precursor essentially in being powered by an Armstrong Siddeley Viper 2 turbojet, for which air intakes are positioned on the fuselage sides in way of the cockpit enclosure. The main undercarriage is of the nosewheel type and has been made retractable. A Naval deck-landing version is also in mind.'

Flight International, September 1953 p.300.

As is traditional with any military contract, the projected cost increased piecemeal, until by 1955 it had reached £250,000, an absolute fortune in today's terms. The 'little juggling' hinted at by Bryan Knight was actually more like major surgery. Firstly there was the conversion from a piston to jet-power plant, and naturally not everyone had the same view on where this should be mounted. The preliminary design

The Jindivik and development of the Jet Provost were inextricably linked throughout the late 1950s. (Courtesy Mark Pengellie, Aberporth)

simply removed the Leonides from the front of the airframe and replaced it with the jet under a fairing, with a hole in the centre acting as an intake. The jet pipes were to be mounted either side of the lower fuselage. Luckily this was quickly discarded in favour of a more conventional 'straight through' layout, the only departure being the bifurcated duct, drawing air in from two intakes on the lower forward fuselage. The power plant chosen was the Armstrong Siddeley Viper ASV-5, a derivative of the small compact turbojet originally designed as a short life ECU for the Jindivik target drone.

VIPER

The story of the Viper can be traced back to discussions between the Ministry of Supply and the Australian Department of Supply & Development held in London in 1948. The immediate post-war period saw a rapid increase in missile development, especially air-to-air, forcing the development of aerial target vehicles that could perform like an enemy fast jet. That initial meeting set in motion the development of the Jindivik – '*The Hunted*' in Aboriginal. The vehicle airframe and flight systems were designed and built by the Australian General Aircraft Factory (GAF), whilst Armstrong Siddeley Motors won the contract to construct a compact, short-life power plant. The first built version of the Viper, a ASV-2, successfully ran on the company's test bed at the beginning of 1951, and by November the first production engine had passed the ten-hour test stage required by the Ministry. From there the engine was test-flown in the company's Lancaster flight test-bed aircraft before being shipped to Australia for installation in the Jindivik. Development of the long-life version of the engine, the ASV-5, began in early 1953, and by November the first had completed 150 hours at maximum rpm. The ASV-5 was selected by a number of companies including Folland to power the Midge, but it was with the proposed Hunting Percival trainer that the engine and later derivatives found its biggest market.

The Viper was mounted in the old cockpit, forward of the original rear bulkhead and above the main spar. Two large engine doors and a removable central beam took the place of the transparencies. The cockpit was moved forward with the rear bulkhead now aligned with the mainplane leading edge. This was, in turn, fitted with a streamline nose to house the battery, radios, and instrumentation; later this would include oxygen bottles as well. The two intakes were fitted to the sides of the cockpit structure, forward of the wing leading edge. Moving the cockpit forward, just over three feet and moving the heavy engine to a more central position entirely changed the aircraft's centre of gravity. Luckily, with no propeller in the way less ground clearance was required, and consequently the tail wheel was substituted for one at the nose. This had the added bonus of giving a more effective thrust direction, with the jet efflux being expelled perpendicular to the direction of travel. The problem was that the span of the propeller had dictated the length of the main undercarriage, and as the object of the exercise was to keep cost to a minimum, it was cheaper to fit a nose leg that complimented the existing mains, rather than completely redesign the system. Eventually a shock strut with the correct extension was located; bizarrely it was actually a slightly modified Bristol Sycamore leg. The consequent tricycle arrangement meant that the only way to access the aircraft cockpit was via a set of 'A' frame steps. The undercarriage arrangement also gave rise to some interesting taxiing characteristics, especially on grass, as the aircraft crabbed and wandered around alarmingly.

The wing remained essentially the same, apart from strengthening across the rear spar to withstand the pressures exerted when the new spoilers were deployed. The lower surface was redesigned between the spars to accommodate a retractable

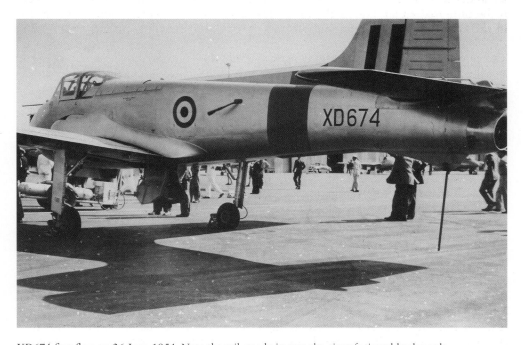

XD674 first flew on 26 June 1954. Note the tail-steady in case the aircraft tipped backwards.

undercarriage. Both these improvements were essential to the operation of the new jet arrangement. By re-engining the aircraft over 100mph extra had been achieved in performance, and the aircraft had a potential to reach in excess of 400mph, twice that of the Leonides powered Provost. Naturally the streamlining of the aircraft was paramount, and consequently a retractable undercarriage was fitted, powered by a pneumatic system. The increase in speed and reduction in drag also necessitated the spoiler fit, again pneumatically powered. The empennage was identical to that used on the piston T.Mk.1. The rear fuselage was increased cross-sectionally to accommodate the jet pipe and externally had a small ventral fin, running the length of the lower surface. This was to reduce the adverse yaw caused by the increase of frontal area the cockpit reconstruction had caused.

By the beginning of 1954 stories of the new aircraft were being keenly followed in the aviation press. Only one thing was missing – a name. The project had originally been called the Percival Jet Trainer, but since early 1953 'Jet Provost' had been bandied about. Over Christmas 1953 one of the design team came up with a name that encompassed all the aircraft was about. It began with a 'P', keeping the Percival tradition alive and signified the primary role of the aircraft. However, the Percival 'Primus' just didn't have the same bite as the Jet Provost, and in February 1954 it was announced that 'Jet Provost' would remain.

On 26 June 1954 following a series of engine runs, Hunting's Chief Test Pilot Dick Wheldon piloted the first flight in XD674 (Constructor's number PAC/84/001) from

XD676 the first 'production' model T.Mk.1 flew in April 1955. Note the undercarriage length and the aircraft being on grass. At this time training aircraft, including the Jet Provost, were required to operate from grass strips.

Luton. It was so successful a further seven flights were made over the next three days. Further proving flights and more ambitious manoeuvres followed, including an impromptu wheels-up landing on 18 July – luckily only minor damage occurred. The aircraft was soon repaired and by September that year was being demonstrated at the Society of British Aircraft Constructors (SBAC) showcase at Farnborough.

The aircraft was extensively tested by the manufacturer at Luton before being flown to A&AEE at Boscombe Down for Ministry of Supply trials that November. However, in August 1954, after 123 hours, Hunting Percival were laying claim to some interesting operating costs, enticing potential orders with some impressive figures:

'It is claimed that, making all due allowances for initial first cost of the aircraft, upkeep of airfields, unit equipment, maintenance and overhaul costs, spares backings, etc., the Jet Provost can be operated at £61 per flying hour, whereas an advanced trainer (of unspecified type) costs £161 per flying hour. These figures are based on 30-week instructional courses covering 120 hours' flying on each aircraft. In the opinion of some training staff officers at least 30 hours of the advanced stage syllabus can be handled by the Jet Provost, resulting in a saving of £3,000 per pupil on flying casts alone. Remembering a recent Parliamentary answer, in which it was stated that to train a bomber pilot now costs something like £25,000, such an economy is of considerable significance.'

'Jet Provost Performance' *Flight International*, 6 August 1954.

XD674 T.Mk.1. The forward probe allowed for accurate indicated airspeed and allowed side-slip to be indicated. The undercarriage was a mixture of the original Provost mains and a Bristol Sycamore nose leg!

WHITE MICE

The first of three aircraft placed on charge, known as 'Phase A', arrived at CFS Little Rissington in June 1955, where QFIs immediately set about designing a new course syllabus. Handling qualities were also studied during this phase, and firm recommendations were made in the aircraft's favour after only 111 hours of flying. A further six aircraft, 'Phase B', forming the second part of the Ministry-sponsored RAF assessment programme, were dispatched to No.2 FTS, under the command of Gp Capt R.J. Abrahams, at Hullavington in August 1955. These aircraft formed the core of the flying tuition course. The student pilots, known to the CFS instructors as the 'White Mice' (blind leading the blind!) were not selected specifically for the evaluation. Rather, they were the next course due to start *ab initio* training, and just happened to be assigned the Jet rather than Piston Provost. This gave a far more accurate picture of both the aircrafts' performance in the hands of student pilots, and also allowed the timings to be more realistically monitored. The first student solo took place on 17 October 1955 after 8hr 20mins of instruction. Taking an average across fifty students, CFS suggested at least 1hr 30mins could be shaved off the time it took before the first solo flight, a considerable annual saving in the training budget. Phase B was complete on 2 July 1956 by which time 2,258 hours had been flown with very few unserviceabilities.

Of course a new aircraft always raises interest, especially from the ground crew, and the T.Mk.1 was no exception. Given the fact it was slightly ungainly it raised a few eyebrows as well:

"At South Cerney three of them visited us on one occasion and I was told that the RAF was evaluating them. – I thought "Oh my God – what a lash-up". There they stood on their long, spindly legs and powered (so we were told) by an engine designed to have a twenty-four hour life and was intended for a missile! You appreciate that S.C. was a grass field so, on taxying the u/c flexed quite noticeably. The u/c, and presumably the flaps, was pneumatically operated as far as I can remember, meaning that if you blinked while watching one take off, you almost certainly missed seeing the retraction – it was that quick."

Bryan Beames

And it wasn't all plain sailing during the evaluation either.

'In our memorandum to you on the 25th October 1955, we concluded from our examination that the fire and explosion was due to the spontaneous ignition of free fuel in the rear fuselage. This free fuel most probably originated from the air relief valve when the vent system filled with fuel during aerobatics. The main contributory factor to the fire and explosion was the collection of this free fuel in the rear fuselage. The inefficient venting system discharge point and inadequate sealing of the skinning permitted this free fuel to enter the rear fuselage and ventral fin.'

Accident to Jet Provost XD680 on 1-9-55, Accidents Investigation Branch, 15 November 1956 (PRO (AVIA 5/34)).

Dramatic as this sounded, the aircraft was soon back on the evaluation programme. The problem of free fuel igniting in the rear fuselage of aircraft was not a new phenomenon, as the AIB readily noted. Similar problems had been encountered in Vampire, Venom and Hunter aircraft, and this had been partially rectified by the

XD680 T.Mk.1 on the ramp at Hullavington. The aircraft suffered a jet pipe fire in (Oct 1955); however, repairs ensured the aircraft was returned to service. (Bigbird Aviation)

G-AOBU T.Mk.1. Percival Aircraft's own private demonstrator. (Percival Aircraft)

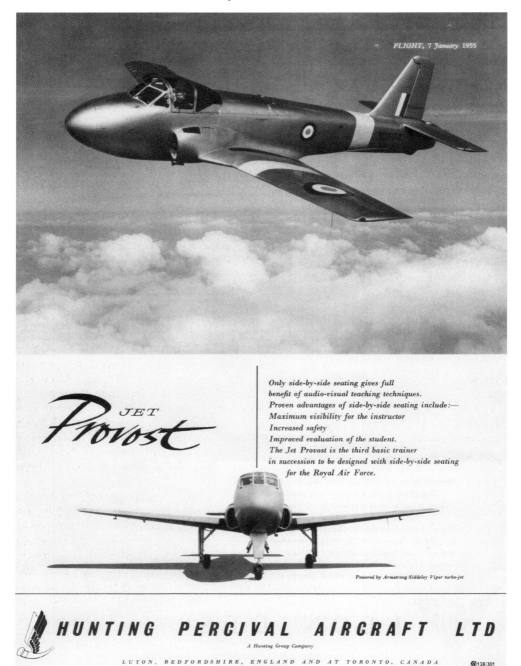

The T.Mk.1 enters service. (Flight International)

addition of suction vents. This required a series of drain holes to be placed along the underside of the aircraft, which were then fitted with suction fairings. The idea was that the fairing induced a negative pressure below the drain and sucked out any residual fuel and vapours. Other issues showed up during the programme. The T.Mk.1 undercarriage flaps and airbrakes were all serviced by a pneumatic operating system. Throughout the winter 1955-56 temperatures were unexpectedly low, and even more so when flying. Consequently, the pneumatic system devised by Dunlop suffered a number of failures due to icing. From the T.Mk.2 all services were hydraulically operated, removing both the problem of icing and the majority of other snags experienced on the T.Mk.1s. These were, however, teething problems and by 8 February 1957 CFS was reporting in an Air Ministry News Statement that the project was a resounding success:

"The first [Jet Provost] course was tested by the Examining Wing of the Central Flying School and the Examining Wing of the NATO Air Training Advisory Group. Both concluded that it had attained a considerably higher standard of pilot ability than piston-trained students at an equivalent stage. The C.F.S. examining team commented on student standards as follows: 'Compared with the average student trained on the Piston Provost the jet-trained students have, in a shorter time in the air, achieved a more dexterous and better mental approach to the art of modern flying. Their repertoire of aerobatic manoeuvres, for example, is generally much more extensive and flown with much more accuracy and spirit."

In March 1957 *Flight International* visited Hullavington to check on developments; the programme was then eighteen months old. By then No.2 FTS had flown the aircraft for 4,000 hours and performed 11,000 landings. In that time the servicing hours had been reduced to nearly one hour for one hour flying time and it was considered that that should be lower, once the more ground crew-friendly T.Mk.2 came on line. So, by early 1957 it was clear that 'all-through jet training' was the way forward. The RAF continued to develop course timings, and by the end of November 1957 over 7,023 hours had been logged on the type, over 6,000 of which had been in the hands of students.

On 29 January the Ministry of Supply had received Treasury approval to place a provisional order for 100 T.Mk.3 aircraft. Development now started in earnest on a successor to the T.Mk.1 Jet Provost that was, after all, no more than a thrown-together concept aircraft. With a firmer commitment towards development, the future looked secure for Hunting Percival – nothing could have been further from the truth. The company was used to name changes, when the project had first been discussed it was as Percival Aircraft Ltd, actually a subsidiary of Hunting Aircraft from 1944. By the time of the first flight this had changed to Hunting Percival Ltd, as the owners made their presence felt. Percival was dropped altogether when in 1957 the company became Hunting Aircraft Ltd. But within a few years it was to face total extinction, as the Government sought to rationalize the landscape of the British aerospace industry.

T.Mk.2

Whilst the training value of the Jet Provost was being evaluated by Central Flying School and the Ministry of Supply, Hunting Percival was devising a series of test aircraft designed to take the concept through to production. On 1 September 1955, the substantially redesigned T.Mk.2 aircraft took to the skies. Only four of the type

XD694. T.Mk.2. A redesigned T.Mk.1, one immediate improvement was the redesign of the undercarriage arrangement.

were to do so. The contract for further development had been placed by the Treasury in June 1955 for one T.Mk.2 aircraft to serve with the RAF as an evaluation test-bed, at an estimated cost of £109,000. Hunting produced three further airframes, two as private venture company demonstrators that were destined to travel extensively, the third played a pivotal role in the development of the next generation T.Mk.3.

MODS

From a distance the aircraft looked substantially the same, and in certain respects that was true; however, some areas were radically different. The T.Mk.2 was a development aircraft not a conceptual one as the T.Mk.1 had been. Consequently, many system developments had been introduced. Primary and most noticeable was the redesign of the undercarriage. Out went the gangly, thrown-together pneumatically actuated arrangement, replaced by a purpose-built hydraulically operated layout. The two main legs were reduced-length direct action oleo, whilst the new nose leg was a lever-suspension liquid spring. Lowering the aircraft by an incredible twenty-two inches made it more stable whilst taxiing and meant that the groundcrew no longer needed 'A' frame ladders just to reach the walkway on the wing or refuel. The T.Mk.1 had been fitted with a mechanical steering system, taken directly off the rudder bar; this coupled with the length of the nose leg had led to some difficulties, especially on grass. The arrangement was replaced with a toe brake system, allowing for differential braking. One small problem came when the aircraft needed to stop. On the majority of other aircraft a column-mounted handle, similar to that found on a bicycle, was

XD694 T.Mk.2 undergoing certification trials at A&AEE Boscombe Down.

fitted. When the crew wanted to stop they simply squeezed the handle. The Jet Provost needed the application of both toe brakes. Naturally, experienced crews found this a little disconcerting, and the students had to be taught the old way of swinging the rudder bar when applying the brakes to prepare them for their 'advanced training'.

The fuselage also received attention. On the T.Mk.1 a ventral fin had been fitted, to counter the adverse yaw due to the increased forward area; now the opportunity was taken to remove that. The entire rear fuselage as far back as the jet pipe shroud was reshaped, to give both a smoother contour and more satisfactory clearance for the jet pipe. XD694 received its Service Release Certificate on 6 September 1956 after 143 hours flying with Hunting from Luton, and a further 45 hours at A&AEE Boscombe Down. Whilst at Boscombe Down some major modifications to the cockpit area were recommended, including the addition of an ejector seat for both crewmembers and a clear visibility windscreen and canopy. Cockpit modifications required the introduction of a far more effective anti-icing system, the problem of widescreen and canopy icing having been encountered whilst flying at height. The Treasury allotted £165,000 in January 1957 to cover the work, hoping it would be money well spent, as the modifications would become production standard with the T.Mk.3. By 1958, XD694 had joined the T.Mk.1s at Hullavington. A further 260 hours were clocked up at the hands of QFIs and students, before the aircraft joined Armstrong Siddeley on engine development.

> 'The engine for this aircraft is the Viper 8, which is a development of the basic Viper engine for the Jindivik. Expenditure over the next three years on the Viper as a whole is estimated at £530,000.'

Ministry of Supply AirB2(a), Jet Provost Mark 3, 29 January 1957. (PRO T 225/810)

By late 1957 engine development testing had started in earnest for the new generation T.Mk.3. The T.Mk.1 had been powered by the Viper 5; however, an increase of thrust and greater engine reliability led to the development of the Viper 8. The engine was fitted to XD694 and put through a 150-hour flying programme at the Armstrong Siddeley Motors Ltd (ASM) airfield at Bitteswell. The test report issued on 22 April 1958 allows the infrastructure of such programmes to be described in some detail. Pilots from A&AEE Boscombe Down, Hunting Aircraft Ltd, and several from ASM carried out the flying. It took the team eleven weeks to complete the 150 hours considered long enough to prove the mechanical reliability of the development engine. Flight testing commenced on 18 December 1957 and was completed by 4 March 1958, '*Flying was not undertaken on any Saturday or Sunday or the Christmas Holiday period.*' Noted the test report. To ensure maintenance and other minor unservicabilities did not interrupt the programme, all rectification and inspection work was undertaken by a night shift. Initial tests were a success, leading to a proposal to retest the aircraft with a single engine for 500 hours development flying later that year. With such test programmes the unexpected often appears, and this was no exception. The aircraft's hydraulic system was supplied by an Engine Driven Pump (EDP) and naturally any engine-powered component was included in the programme. As part of the test sequences the undercarriage was cycled at various heights, inducing a loading on the EDP and changing the dynamics of the airframe.

> '6.0 Aircraft Serviceability
> The only work required to maintain the airframe serviceable during the period of the test that was not covered during the periods allotted for daily servicing was concerned with the replacement of undercarriage hydraulic pipes. Fracture of these pipes followed the lowering of the undercarriage in flight at 25,000 feet (ambient temperature -50°C). Temporary replacement pipes were manufactured at ASM pending the supply of the correct pipes from Huntings.'

Report on the 150-hour Development Flight Testing of Viper 8 Engine V.1505 in Hunting MkII Jet Provost XD.694 (April 1958)

THE PRIVATE VENTURE FLEET

Private venture aircraft were a legacy of the early days of aircraft manufacture. Indeed, Charles Gardner in his history of the British Aircraft Corporation nicely summed the situation up, '*The days of knocking up quick, cheap, private-venture prototypes in the experimental hangar were over.*' Today the construction of a concept aircraft, virtually modelled and flown through computer simulation, costs aerospace companies many thousands if not millions of pounds, and all this before the aircraft is built. As we have seen the P.56 was built as a private venture as was the conversion to a P.84; however, this was to be one of the last successful types to do so. When XD694 was taken off the T.Mk.1 line and heavily modified, it was financed by the Treasury, which by now had expressed more than a passing interest in the basic jet trainer. Sensing potential worldwide sales, Hunting Percival built a further two T.Mk.2 company demonstrators, naturally capitalizing on the Treasury-financed design.

During the early months of 1958, flight tests were conducted in the first of the two civil registered T.Mk.2s - G-AOUS. The tests had two objectives: to provide general information on fatigue loading of the tailplane and fin, and to provide information for assessing the fatigue life of the proposed T.Mk.3 '- *in its future role as a basic trainer for the RAF.*' Various flight and ground conditions were monitored, according to information obtained from CFS at Little Rissington and Hullavington. Those early operating conditions are worth repeating here:

> 'It was estimated from information obtained that a typical flying course on a Jet Provost comprises the following operations:- 330 take-offs and landings, 10% on grass and the rest on metalled surfaces; 19 hours taxying with the same division between grass and metalled surfaces; 101 hours flight at various heights and speeds, for 5.5 hours of which the airbrakes are open; and 220 aerobatics including 62 spins.'

'Fatigue Loadings in Flight.' Tech Note No. Structures 260, February 1959.

All testing required on grass was carried out at White Waltham Aerodrome, whilst those needing a metalled surface were done at RAE Farnborough. During taxying on a hard surface the tailplane had a very low load reading; however, as the aircraft 'bounced' along on the grass the load was very noticeably increased. But without doubt the most severe loading was when the aircraft was in the spin. And this was greatly increased by the manoeuvring loads imposed by the pilot trying to correct it.

By late 1958 an up-rated version of the Viper engine, giving a new take-off rating based on 13,800rpm, had been developed. Interestingly, this had not been designed

G-AOUS T.Mk.2 on static display at Farnborough. The aircraft still sported the 'piston' segmented windscreen. This received major criticism from Ministry pilots.

with the Jet Provost in mind. Just as the AS Viper 5 (powering the T.Mk.1) had been developed from the first generation short-life GAF Jindivik engine, so the Viper 11 was designed for the new Mks of Jindivik. G-AOUS was dispatched to Bitteswell and retro fitted with the new engine in May 1959. Assessment flights were undertaken in the first two weeks of June with the test programme including speed trials in straight and level flight.

Tests, again at Bitteswell, revealed a slight problem with the jet pipe cooling system. All Jet Provost had two ram air ducts on the upper engine doors either side of the spine, to allow a constant stream of ambient temperature air through the engine compartment and down the tail structure surrounding the jet pipe. When on the ground, the temperature was controlled by the extraction effect set up by the jet efflux, effectively drawing air through the ducts and over the lagged jet pipe. The rear section of the aircraft, essentially the empennage, was protected from temperature by a stainless steel shroud known as the 'nib'. In an attempt to negate a drop in temperature of around thirty-five degrees Celsius caused by the shroud, the tail pipe was extended, and to save time the shroud was not refitted during ground runs; however:

> 'Since with the shroud in position and extended nozzle fitted the limiting temperature at one of the aircraft rear frames was reached following engine shut-down, it was thought inadvisable to repeat the ground run with the shroud removed.'

Aircraft and Engine Performance Tests on a Jet Provost fitted with a Viper 11 Engine Bristol Siddeley Engines. Report No.V.11/1, June 1959.

Subsequently the shroud was redesigned, appearing as the familiar shape that spawned its nick-name. Unfortunately other parts of the trials did not go so well:

> 'These tests afforded the first opportunity for studying the performance of the Viper 11 in flight as part of the engine development programme prior to the installation of the Viper 11 in the Jindivik. Owing to the influence of the jet pipe cooling system on the performance of the engine, the consistency of the results was not as good as expected compared with previous work conducted on Viper 8 Provost installations.'

Aircraft and Engine Performance Tests on a Jet Provost Fitted with a Viper 11 Engine. Bristol Siddeley Engines. Report No.V.11/1, June 1959.

However, it was not a total loss as the installation of the Viper 11 had demonstrated the aircraft was capable of much greater things, paving the way for the fastest model ever produced – the T.Mk.4. G-AOUS spent the rest of the year in Portuguese colours whilst their air force evaluated a number of airframes as a potential trainer.

SPREADING THE WORD

With the RAF expressing more than a passing interest in the aircraft and requesting the development of more advanced aircraft, it was clear that other air forces might well be interested in the concept of 'all through jet training'. With this in mind the other company Private Venture Aircraft, G-AOHD, embarked on two extensive sales initiatives in an attempt to prove the aircrafts effectiveness to other markets.

G-AOHD

G-AOHDs varied career started with a demonstration tour across the South American continent and was swiftly followed by a spell in Australia. The aircraft was crated and shipped out to Trinidad in February 1958. By April 21 it had flown the first proving flight after Ashby and Ashley; the two supporting engineers had reconstructed it. The hot conditions, reaching 96deg F. on occasion, allowed take-off and climb performance to be assessed and wired back to the United Kingdom. On 28 April Hunting test pilot R.N. Rumbelow flew to Caracas, Venezuela, covering 340nm at 25,000ft. From 28 April to 7 May the aircraft was demonstrated to Air Force officers at Maracay, before flying to Bogata, Columbia, in three overnight stops. After providing flights for the Columbians, the aircraft flew to the airfield at Quito in Ecuador, where at an altitude of over 10,000ft. the aircraft performed perfectly. During the first two weeks of June, after crossing the Andes Mountain range, the aircraft provided an extensive evaluation programme. The Peruvian authorities requested that two part-trained and three complete novice students undergo the proposed training scheme. *'Tuition was exceptionally concentrated'*, reported *Flight* International in November 1958, *'The statistics – one aeroplane, two instructors, five pupils, 55 hours, two weeks, speak for themselves; they almost certainly constitute some kind of record!'*

By 28 June the aircraft had arrived in Chile, providing ten flights for Air Force Officers. Five days later, Rumbelow was crossing the Andes again at 25,000 ft, arriving in Mendoza Argentina where displays and flights for both Air Force and Navy pilots were conducted. On the 19 July the aircraft arrived in Uruguay, flying test pilots, pilots and instructors from Carrasco Airfield. The final leg of the incredible journey was into Brazil, terminating at Rio de Janeiro. As a final gesture, Rumbelow was given special permission to perform his aerobatic display over the world-famous Copacabana Beach to thousands of onlookers. By 12 August, the aircraft was already being crated up for the long journey back to Luton. G-AOHD had flown 8,400 miles

G-AOHD T.Mk.2. This company demonstrator travelled extensively on sales tours.

G-AOHD T.Mk.2. The aircraft was assigned to the Royal Australian Air Force for trials. Numbered A99-001, it was deemed uneconomical to repatriate the aircraft. It is the only T.Mk.2 to survive, residing in an Australian museum.

across nine countries, spending 178 hours in the air. The aircraft operated from 27 airfields, landing 630 times and carrying 123 passengers. After such an arduous programme it was inevitable that the aircraft suffered some unserviceabilities; however, the measure of faith placed in the aircraft's expected performance can be judged by the spares requirement:

'- with only two suitcases of spares, the aircraft carried on consistently day in and day out. One instrument was replaced, two navigation light filaments, a pair of rubber seals in the brakes, one flap interconnecting rod and two mainwheel tyres. A welding repair was effected on the jet tail cone at Montevideo.'

Jet Provost Odyssey' *Flight International*, 21 November 1958.

The South American tour was not the end of G-AOHD's travels. In 1959 the aircraft was given an Australian tail serial (A99-001) and shipped out under the request of the RAAF, which was interested in implementing all-through jet training. The aircraft was incorporated into No.35 Pilot Training Course at No.1 Basic Flying Training School at Point Cook. Two students were selected to fly the Jet Provost, whilst the remainder were tutored on the Winjeel, a basic two seat aircraft not unlike the Piston Provost. Unfortunately the RAAF deemed the jet aircraft an unnecessary expense and consequently made no order. At the end of the six-month trial and with the aircraft effectively redundant, it was presented to Sydney Technical College as an instructional airframe. The aircraft still resides in Australia and is the sole survivor of the T.Mk.2s.

G-23-1 (XN177)

The final T.Mk.2, sometimes referred to as T.Mk.2b, was a true development aircraft. Whilst the other aircraft made their way around the world, G-23-1 flew south-west to the Aircraft & Armament Experimental Establishment (A&AEE) at Boscombe Down, for a Qualitative Preview Handling Assessment. The idea had been to fly a fully representative version of the Mk.3; however, A&AEE ended up with mixture of Mk.2 & 3 components – in the true spirit of Jet Provost development.

'G-23-1 was a development Mk.2 Jet Provost modified to become a reasonably representative aerodynamic prototype of the Mk.3 version, which is destined for Service introduction in quantity as the RAF basic trainer. G-23-1 was sent to this establishment for Preview handling trials in April 1958. The main differences between G-23-1 and the production Mk.3 aircraft were that G-23-1 was not fitted with ejection seats, it had a non-standard cockpit layout and it was fitted with the Mk.2 cockpit sliding hood.'

Jet Provost Prototype T.Mk.3 G-23-1. Qualitative Preview Handling Assessment. AAEE/875/3 April 1958 (AVIA 18/4244)

However, the differences went much further than that, so much so that A&AEE could only cover part of the trial. The wings were taken from the production line rather than following the original Mk.2; this meant that the ailerons were of a different configuration. The tailplane rigging, including the incidence, was non-standard and the fin leading edge had been re-profiled, making it sharper. The most limiting factor was the cockpit, as mentioned in the report:

'Because of these differences, no cockpit assessment or night-flying was undertaken and only limited spinning was done as canopy design was understood to affect the behaviour at entry to, and in, the spin.'

Some items of equipment were clearly nowhere near usable.

'Ice Detector Unit. This unit requires considerable development before it can be regarded as satisfactory. During the trial, the warning light came on in various conditions of flight in clear air and could often be put out by side-slipping the aircraft. It is considered that in its present state it would be a source of confusion and worry to the pupil pilot.'

Jet Provost Prototype T.Mk.3 G-23-1. Qualitative Preview Handling Assessment. AAEE/875/3 April 1958 (AVIA 18/4244)

Not everything was problematic. A new brake system incorporating a servo and improved nose-wheel castoring ensured a far more effective ground handling profile. And it did sport a new two-piece, molded windscreen, rather than the multiple flat plates that were a legacy of the Piston Provost. Modification of the windscreen had been a recommendation on XD694's release to service flights in late 1956, as had the addition of ejection seats. The reasons behind them not being fitted to G-23-1 were to become all too apparent as the aircraft went into production.

XN177 T.Mk.2 on trials at Boscombe Down. This aircraft also took part in hot weather trials in Aden.

ADEN

G-23-1, by now re-serialed XN177, left Boscombe in 1958 to become part of the tropical evaluations trials team deploying to Aden. Interestingly, these weapon trials were conducted during a major incident involving attacking Yemeni tribesmen that had surrounded a British fort at Assarir on 27 April. Naturally the RAF, as part of the British Forces Arabian Peninsula, deployed aircraft in support. Venoms performed numerous ground-attack missions, loosing three to enemy fire. Clearly, something a little more modern was required, and quickly, as unrest had been spreading across the Middle East since the Suez Crisis of 1956.

'A series of tropical evaluation trials of the Folland Gnat, Hawker Hunter and Hunting Jet Provost is shortly to be held by the R.A.F. at Aden. An announcement that such tests were contemplated was made by A.V-M. W. H. Kyle, A.C.A.S. (Operational Requirements), when he spoke on future equipment at the R.A.F. conference "Prospect Two" last month. He said then that while it had become almost a tradition for fighter aircraft well tried in the U.K. to be used for ground attack, defence and tactical reconnaissance needs overseas, modern high performance interceptors were becoming less

XD694 T.Mk.2 was used extensively in the development of the Viper engine.

suitable for this general-purpose role. What was needed was something "simpler, more versatile and more economical." The aircraft on trial will probably be flown by Service pilots.'

'Service Aviation' *Flight International*, 13 June 158, p. 814

Armstrong Siddeley retro-fitted a Viper 9 for the trials, gathering vital hot-weather information for the company's design engineers at home. Clearly the aircraft was no match for the Gnat and Hunter, and, once the trials were over, Hunting seized the opportunity to demonstrate training and ground-attack capabilities. Chief Test Pilot S.B. Oliver, with a two-man support team, R. Brown (sales manager at Hunting), and D. Oxford (Armstrong Siddeley Motors) following in commercial airliners, flew on to Pakistan and India. At Jodhpur, the Indian Air Force requested Hunting run a reduced-flight training course for two instructors and two *ab initio* cadets. The two students had no more than thirty hours on gliders; one failed to make the grade however the other, Flying Cadet Iabal Singh, flew solo after 9½ hours. Whilst with the Indian Air Force, the Viper 9 used for the RAF hot-weather trials was replaced with the more standard Viper 8, helping to demonstrate the simplicity of the aircraft when considering maintenance. Although neither air force placed orders, the concept of an armed version had been more than proven. The next hurdle was to get the aircraft successfully into production.

Building a small fleet of concept aircraft such as the T.Mk.1s and subsequently modifying that design for the T.Mk.2 was a manageable process for Hunting Percival – but only just. They were about to embark on a major production run, so it was vitally important that all the lessons learnt were put into practice. Unfortunately, it was going to take a lot of public money to do it.

3.

'The best aircraft for the purpose'.

On 26 June 1959, the Royal Air Force proudly took delivery of their first Jet Provost T.Mk.3. It was almost five years to the day since the rather ungainly T.Mk.1 (XD674) had taken to the skies over Luton. What had started out as a cheap private venture project had culminated in an initial order for 100 aircraft. It was a major achievement, and one that was set to continue well beyond the life of the company. By 1960, the aircraft had become an integral feature of the RAF's training capability, representing both the service and individual Flying Training Schools at many events. Within three years two further marks had appeared, complimenting the comprehensive scheme. The political, production, and financial background of the T.Mk.3, and subsequent T.Mk.4, is the subject of this chapter.

At the end of January 1957, the Treasury approved the request made by the Ministry of Supply for an order for 100 Mk.3 aircraft, subject to the inclusion of certain specifications. One major point was the inclusion of ejection seats, a recommendation that had been made at A&AEE during the trials of the T.Mk.2. However Hunting Percival was not as keen, as was to become all too apparent later.

On 8 February 1957 the newly appointed Secretary of State for Air, George Ward, announced in the House of Commons:

> 'The evaluation trials have shown that ab initio flying training on jet aircraft has definite advantages, and it has therefore been decided to establish this form of training on a larger scale. A production order is being placed for the Jet Provost, which I am satisfied is the best aircraft for the purpose.'

A month later, during the vote on Air Force Service (7 March 1957) the decision was applauded by The Right Hon. P.B. Lucas, member for Brentford & Chiswick:

> 'The production order for this aircraft, after the basic decision had been taken was, to all intents and purposes, inevitable and I consider it to have been quite proper.'

He went on:

> 'Having said that, however, I must now ask my right hon. Friend not to disregard, even at this late stage, the possibility of the Miles M.100, not only in the form which will soon fly, but also in the projected Mark III version, which is very much in mind.'

The Miles M100 Student was the only real completion for the training aircraft contract, unfortunately it was three years too late.

The Miles M.100 was designed and built as a private venture aircraft, and the company was not without its supporters in Government. Lucas, clearly with some interest in the company, pointed out '-*it comes, after all, from a stable which designed and developed about 7,000 training aircraft between 1938 and 1946, in addition to some of the best light aircraft which the country has ever known.*'

Development had started back in 1953, when Miles discovered the representations being made at Government-level by Percival staff. Naturally, production of a two-seat trainer was well within the capabilities of the firm, and by the end of the year a clear way forward for a brand new design had been tabled. The aircraft was powered by the Turbomeca Marbore turbojet, giving a maximum speed of nearly 300mph, with a ceiling of 20,000ft. The aircraft first flew on 15 May 1957, but by then it was already too late, almost three years too late in fact. Consequently Miles missed out on any orders for the M.100 'Student', as it was by now optimistically called; however, undeterred, they sought other markets, specifically the Counter-Insurgency (COIN) role being demanded by many Governments by the early 1960s. Unfortunately, the Jet Provost in its armed Mk.50s variants and the later Strikemaster was to ensure that only one such aircraft was built.

What is interesting to our account of the Jet Provost is the phenomenon of 'private venture'. The fact that the P.56 Provost and P.84 Jet Provost were both private ventures has already been covered, and it should come as no surprise to the reader that other companies were also designing and constructing aircraft in a similar, speculative way. However, change was on the horizon, primarily in the form of missiles – or so the Government hoped.

'ROCKETS'

In 1957 the then Minister of Defence, Duncan Sandys, published a White Paper on Defence that remains notorious to this day. So swathing was it in its reductions across the military establishment that is was to change the landscape of British aviation forever. Not least because it dictated that aircraft manufactures would need to collaborate or die. The White Paper received major media coverage around the world:

> 'With an almost audible sigh of relief, Great Britain last week laid down its role of policeman to the world, and in one bold step advanced into the nuclear age, where its troops will be fewer, its weapons deadlier, and its costs lower. In doing so, Britain almost gratefully abandoned its claim, which has sounded increasingly hollow even to British ears, to rank with the world's two major powers.'

Time Magazine, April 1957.

However, many had missed the point. For two years the Macmillan Government had been struggling with an ever-increasing defence budget, driven in part by the increasing complexities of the many development programmes in place by the mid-1950s. Something clearly had to give and contrary to popular belief, whilst the reduction of the armed services was dramatic, it was not as catastrophic as the Opposition predicted. Increased production in major industries such as steel, coal and motor cars had led to a rise in wages, export earnings and investment. As the economy continued its strong path, the reduction of armed personnel by around 300,000, including the end of National Service by 1960, was hardly noticed.

Key to this reduction was the continued development of missile and nuclear technologies, especially rockets, as Sandys liked to call them. The White Paper had merely echoed what the western world had already become acutely aware of: that there was no protection against a hydrogen bomb attack. Subsequently the whole structure of how Britain would prepare for war radically changed from top to bottom. It is worth considering Macmillan's own words on the subject.

> 'We admitted that Britain and, indeed, Western Europe could not be effectively protected against nuclear attack. The over-riding principle, therefore, must be to prevent war, rather than prepare for it. Accordingly aircraft of Fighter Command were to be substantially reduced, their role in the United Kingdom being limited to defending the deterrent bases. We hoped that they too would in due course be replaced by a system of ground to air guided missiles. The means of delivery of the deterrent which we ourselves manufactured were mainly the V-class bombers which would remain in service for many years.'

Riding the Storm 1956-1959 Harold Macmillan, page 264.

Just a month after the publication of Sandys report, the Government demonstrated its resolve in the construction of a credible nuclear deterrent. The first of a number of two-stage designs, designated '*Short Granite*' was dropped from a Vickers Valiant at the test range at Malden, proving the potential of a home built-hydrogen device. On 8 November 1957 it was demonstrated – 3 megatons of it – at Christmas Island.

In Bedford on 20 July, during a twenty-five years service anniversary for the Tory MP for Mid-Bedfordshire, Mr Lennox-Boyd, the Prime Minister spoke of economic miracles. Major industrial output had led to a substantial rise in export earnings, wages and national investment. *'Indeed let us be frank about it - most of our people have never had it so good'*. Unfortunately, this optimism did not extend to the British Aviation community; by the Farnborough Air Show that September the writing was already on the wall for some companies. Conversely, the future of the Jet Provost as a training aircraft appeared sound:

> 'These and other considerations, which I cannot go into now, lead me to the conclusion that the changeover to guided weapons of one form or another will neither be swift nor yet will it be absolute. That is my view. It will, I think, be a gradual process, with the missile being integrated by degrees into the conventional defences of Fighter Command. And when the guided weapon has taken over certain aircraft responsibilities there will still be many vital roles and uses for which conventional aircraft will still have to be provided.'

7 March 1957, Secretary of State for Air, George Ward, Vote A. Number for Air Force Service. Commons Sitting. Hansard.

Towards Rationalisation

Now is an appropriate time to pause and consider the dynamics of not just Hunting Percival, but that of the whole aerospace industry after WWII. Naturally, during the war aircraft design and construction centred on mass production, sometimes widely dispersed as with the Mosquito and Spitfire, but in all cases rapidly producing the end product. In 1946 there were thirty-five companies whose primary concern was the design and construction of aircraft, complimented by over 800 subsidiary firms providing components. Surprisingly, this was far more extensive than the United States.

By the middle of the 1950s research and development costs far outstripped any potential profit expectations, and most companies were struggling. Three main factors drove the situation. The length of time taken to develop a new aircraft was now so protracted that projects frequently outlived the Government that first commissioned them. This placed them squarely in the firing line when the incoming administration looked for budget savings. Extended development naturally cost more and so increased the cost of each aircraft after development. Consequently, the customer, usually the Government, often with a limited purse, could only cover the cost of a reduced production run. Further, post-war labour costs in Britain had been substantially lower than in America. However, as Britain basked in the sunshine of *'never having it so good'*, inflation was on the increase, leading to higher wage demands, and by the early 1960s this advantage had been totally lost.

In February 1954, the Under Secretary for the Ministry of Supply, Denis Haviland, argued that the policy of spreading orders and development contracts across all the aircraft manufacturers was unsustainable. It made more sense for larger, more robust groups of companies to work together on projects, than for all compete for the work. The V-Force demonstrated how fragmented the situation had become. When viewed objectively, contracts issued for the Vulcan, Victor & Valiant were a serious waste of manufacturing resources, especially in the R&D phase. The triple split order served to sustain three major production companies, and to a greater extent the personalities that ran them. Had they worked together, the cost to the nation would have been a fraction of that actually endured. However, this is where the next late-twentieth century phenomenon – technology - comes into play. Both Handley Page and Avro had designed extremely advanced aircraft for the role, and there was every possibility that one or other might prove impossible to build. Consequently, the Ministry ordered

Contracts to build the V-bomber force pushed the British aircraft community (and the Government) to the limit of its manufacturing capacity.

XM346 T.Mk.3. The first aircraft off the production line. By now many of the problems and recommendations from the A&AEE had been rectified.

from both companies as 'insurance' against failure. The Vickers design was initially rejected; however, some extremely hard lobbying and concessions eventually ensured the company was awarded a contract. All three aircraft were extremely effective and performed the deterrent role for the United Kingdom and NATO for over a decade. Unfortunately, the cost was astronomical; however, the Government was unwilling to force major manufacturers into consortiums, primarily due to the re-armament programme that had been initiated by war in Korea. That said, the landscape of aerospace manufactures was already recognizing change when the Government, driven by the Treasury, finally put its foot down.

When in 1957 British European Airlines, itself a nationalised entity, requested a replacement short-haul aircraft for the Herald, the Government demanded an amalgamated bid for the design. Eventually, a consortium comprising de Havilland, Hunting and Fairey won the contract to build the Trident, under the resurrected name Airco (Aircraft Manufacturing Company). The formation of Airco in early 1958 was a watershed; from this point on only consortium bids would prevail. Within a few years the British Aircraft Corporation (BAC) would manifest itself; Jet Provost was to play a surprisingly important part in the Corporation's future viability.

SEATS

Throughout 1958 costs covering the development programme of the T.Mk.3 continued to rise well beyond initial estimations. Not least, the addition of ejection seats, now being fitted as standard, required some pricy modification to the production fleet:

> 'There is a net increase of £50,000 in the items already approved. A major increase occurred on the ejector seat installation; it was only as work progressed that the need for a complete redesign of the fuselage and canopy lines became apparent. This altered the C.G. making it necessary to strengthen the fuselage and to carry out several thousands of hours of stress testing, none of which had been foreseen.'

Ministry of Supply DM.233/645/025. Jet Provost T.Mk.3, 19 January 1959. (PRO T 225/810).

After further digging at a meeting with Mr. N. Craig (officer in charge of the project for the Ministry of Supply) on 17 February 1959, the Treasury discovered the true extent of the work:

> 'We were told that the ejection seat installation was the first of its kind undertaken by the firm. They underestimated the complexities of the task, particularly the changes necessary and the layout of the controls. The increase included the cost of mock ups, the rearrangement of the controls, front fuselage changes and redesign of the canopy. We were assured that the installation was now working properly.'

Ministry of Supply, Jet Provost Mark III, 22 February 1959. (PRO T 225/810).

This should not have been a surprise, as assisted escape systems had been in discussion from the outset of the project. On 2 August 1956, at a meeting chaired by Sqn Ldr D. Giles and attended by the Hunting Percival team in Luton, the subject of crew safety equipment was discussed.

11. PILOTS SEATS

'It is anticipated that there will be a requirement for the Jet Provost to accommodate crew members wearing crash helmets and dinghies. To meet the additional 4" of height thereby involved with the current seating arrangements would necessitate either accepting a large cut-off for pilots or a major alteration to enlarge the cockpit and alter the canopy line. The Firm contended that both problems could be satisfactorily resolved by the lightweight Ejection Seat which they have previously advocated.

'The meeting noted that it was planned to discuss the requirement for Ejection Seats at a Meeting to be held at A.&A.E.E. on 28/8/56., and agreed that this subject should be re-considered after the results of it were known.'

Jet Provost T.Mk.2 – Cockpit Layout Ref. QF 210

Notes were added to the minutes indicating the outcome:

'The Meeting was held as arranged, and made a firm recommendation for the provision of ejector seats. (n.b. Air Staff have now confirmed the requirement for ejection seats in any envisaged quantity production aircraft.).'

The Jet Provost eventually became the recipient of the Martin-Baker Mk.4 seat. A lightweight version of the Mk.3, this system was to save many aircrews over the operating life of the aircraft. The seat, occasionally modified, was never upgraded; however, a rocket-assisted type (Mk.6) was investigated for the Strikemaster (discussed later).

Moreover, the additional expenditure did not stop there. Aircraft development throughout WWII had driven change at a sometimes alarming rate. In 1939 the RAF was still operating biplanes; by the end of the war jet fighters were shooting down the forerunner of the cruise missile – the V1 *'Doodlebug'*. Throughout the 1950s the aerospace industry was becoming ever more complex with every Government *'Operational Requirement'*. The simple fact was that the Cold War arms race was 'hotting up', relying less on overwhelming numbers and more on technological superiority; naturally this superiority filtered down to the most basic aircraft in the fleet. Consequently, the Ministry of Supply had requested that the T.Mk.3 be the recipient of the latest UHF radio, the first of its kind to go directly into a production aircraft. Once again, the legacy of producing private venture aircraft and then not totally revisiting every system bit the Hunting team. The aircraft wiring was not compatible with the new radio, especially the connectors, forcing modifications as the aircraft were on the production line and increasing substantial delays.

Further problems arose during the flight trials work. T.Mk.2 aircraft rented for trials work by the Ministry of Supply were not built to *'Production Standard'* (PS). This meant that for the all-important Certificate of Airworthiness (C of A) to be granted, further sorties would be required, using production airframes. By late 1958 the first and fourth production models had been despatched from Luton to the Wiltshire airfield, to complete the Qualitative Preview Handling Assessment (QPHA) and subsequent C of A. The cost of flight-testing the T.Mk.3s was absorbed into Government funding, as all production aircraft were technically the property of the Air Ministry. The T.Mk.2s were no longer required and had their rental leases cancelled, saving just over £26,000. As is so often the case, the saving was short lived. The production models were a standard cockpit layout, perfect for student pilots but nowhere near adequate for test flying. On assessment at Boscombe Down the

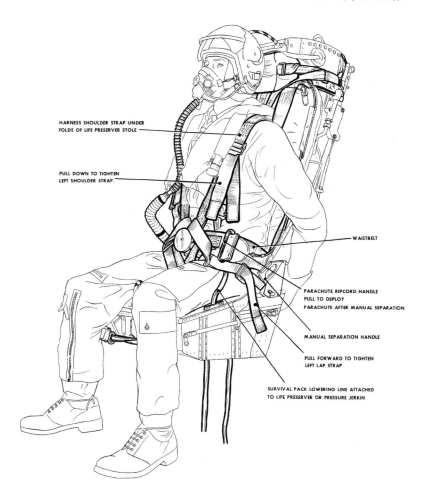

AP 101B-2303A-15
Aircrew Equipment and Oxygen

HARNESS SHOULDER STRAP UNDER
FOLDS OF LIFE PRESERVER STOLE

PULL DOWN TO TIGHTEN
LEFT SHOULDER STRAP.

WAISTBELT

PARACHUTE RIPCORD HANDLE
PULL TO DEPLOY
PARACHUTE AFTER MANUAL SEPARATION

MANUAL SEPARATION HANDLE

PULL FORWARD TO TIGHTEN
LEFT LAP STRAP

SURVIVAL PACK LOWERING LINE ATTACHED
TO LIFE PRESERVER OR PRESSURE JERKIN

1—10 Fig 6 Strapping-in — Sheet 2

1 — 10
Page 11

Above and Opposite: Martin-Baker Ejection seat Mk.4 became standard equipment when the aircraft entered service.

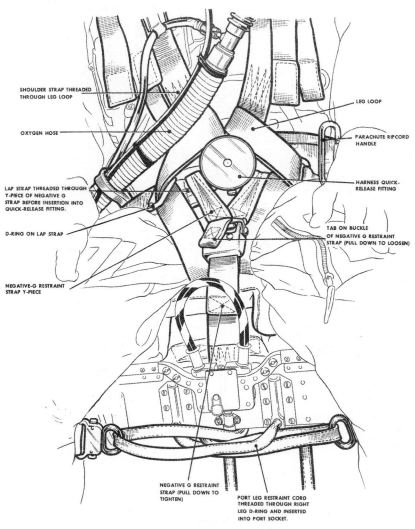

SHOULDER STRAP THREADED
THROUGH LEG LOOP

OXYGEN HOSE

LAP STRAP THREADED THROUGH
Y-PIECE OF NEGATIVE G
STRAP BEFORE INSERTION INTO
QUICK-RELEASE FITTING.

D-RING ON LAP STRAP

NEGATIVE-G RESTRAINT
STRAP Y-PIECE

LEG LOOP

PARACHUTE RIPCORD
HANDLE

HARNESS QUICK-
RELEASE FITTING

TAB ON BUCKLE
OF NEGATIVE G RESTRAINT
STRAP (PULL DOWN TO LOOSEN)

NEGATIVE G RESTRAINT
STRAP (PULL DOWN TO
TIGHTEN)

PORT LEG RESTRAINT CORD
THREADED THROUGH RIGHT
LEG D-RING AND INSERTED
INTO PORT SOCKET.

1—10 Fig 5 Strapping-in

1 — 10
Page 10

This page and opposite: XM346 on trials at Boscombe Down. (MOD)

instrumentation suite was modified for completion of the C of A and QPHA work. Naturally, the Air Ministry did not want 'non-standard' cockpit layouts, and the loaned aircraft were subsequently dispatched on the understanding that any work was rectified before they were returned to the RAF. Unfortunately, this cost the Treasury a further £15,000.

Not too far into the revised trial programme, the undercarriage retraction mechanism on both aircraft produced faults. The flight programme was suspended for two and a half months whilst the Hunting team chased the fault and devised the system modification. As with most problems the design team encountered, the fault was a legacy of the aircraft's thrown-together origins. The shorter, more sensible, undercarriage arrangement first appeared on the T.Mk.2 aircraft and had been successfully tested on the T.Mk.3 development programme. At that time no problem was apparent:

> 'The failure occurred in the mechanical circuit within the aircraft which operates the movement of the undercarriage and its doors. This circuit is a cable operated system embodying a single hydraulic jack. The system is unique to the Jet Provost.'

Ministry of Supply, Jet Provost Mk. 3, (AB/16/01) 13 March 1959. (PRO T 225/810).

Private venture struck again. In an attempt to make the retraction system as cheap as possible, a convoluted collection of components was employed. The hand-built T.Mk.2s had a much higher tolerance and quality of construction than their production successors, and consequently had hidden the systems initial shortcoming, especially in one critical area. The reader will recall that the T.Mk.2 had a slightly different wing to the production T.Mk.3., and whilst the doors had been modified, this had not migrated onto the subsequent construction paperwork. Therefore, when in production the fault was unwittingly built in. The problem was who was going to pay:

> 'This failure of the undercarriage mechanism was most unexpected and puzzling both to the designer and the Department's technical officers. An extremely detailed investigation, including the construction of a test rig, was necessary to determine the cause of the failure and to design measures to safeguard against recurrence.'

Ministry of Supply, Jet Provost Mk. 3, (AB/16/01) 13 March 1959. (PRO T 225/810).

The Treasury was not happy that the Government should shoulder the cost of the modifications, after all '- *this suggested faulty production techniques were the cause of the trouble*'. A subsequent enquiry discovered that designers at Hunting had not acted on their own initiative; technical staff at the Ministry of Supply had approved the modifications to G-23-1. This put the work on an official footing. *'It is unfortunate that this small modification should have led to the need for substantial further development cost, but in the circumstances we see no option but to agree that the Ministry of Supply must bear them.'* The Treasury had no way out and the public purse covered the £15,000 cost of the modification.

By January 1960, eighty-eight T.Mk.3 Jet Provost trainers had been delivered. The production team at Luton was turning out eight aircraft a week, with the prospect of newly engaged staff increasing this to ten shortly. Negotiations for armed versions were in an advanced stage with a number of foreign air forces, and work had been

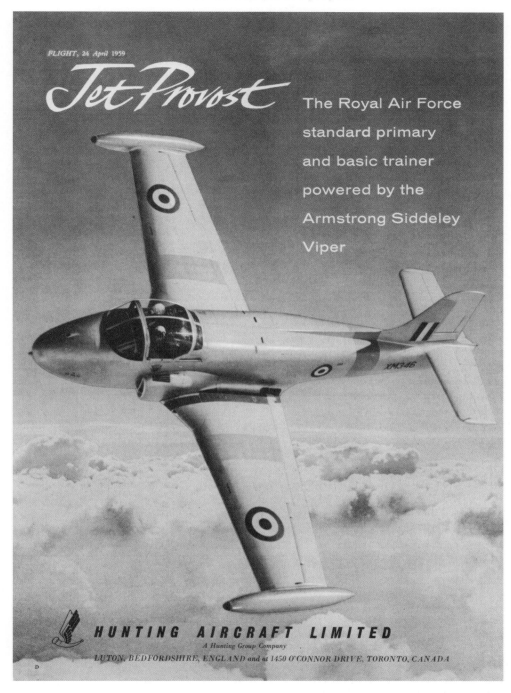

Now the Hunting Group, the company heralds the success of the aircraft. (Flight International)

Jet Provost T.Mk.3s ready for delivery at Luton.

started on the improved T.Mk.4, with a possible 160-aircraft contract with the Government. The future looked good for Hunting Aircraft; however, in boardrooms across the aviation industry an alliance was being hammered out, an alliance that would swallowed up the Jet Provost programme, stamp out the company name and eventually, through increased Government interference, close the Luton factory.

4.

Higher and Faster

The successful introduction of the Jet Provost T.Mk.3 modernised the Royal Air Force almost beyond recognition. Now students were attaining their wings through jet power alone, and the conversion to type at Operational Conversion Units ensured the savings promised had begun to be realised. However, the T.Mk.3 had its limitations, especially in height and speed, both a consequence of the AS Viper 8 powerplant. Nevertheless, the engine manufacturers (by now an amalgamated company known as Bristol Siddeley) knew that, with further development, the Viper had much more to offer. When the Viper 11 made its appearance, a number of aircraft were to benefit, not least the Jet Provost. This chapter charts those benefits through the development of the T.Mk.4 and BAC-145, ultimately to become the T.Mk.5.

The 1961 list of contributors to SBAC Farnborough published by *Flight International* nicely summed up the advantages of the T.Mk.4:

'Jet Provost. In the SBAC flying display this year will be a production Jet Provost T.4 and a production T.51 of the Sudan Air Force will be showing in the static park. The T.51 is an armed version of the Mk 3 trainer now operating in large numbers with the RAF. Powered with a Bristol Siddeley Viper 11 turbojet of 2,500lb thrust—a 40 per cent increase over the Viper in the Mk 3—the Jet Provost T.4 can climb nearly twice as fast as its predecessor, which it will soon begin to supplement in RAF service. A height of 30,000ft is attained in 12.5 min, and the makers report that this remarkably improved performance has been achieved without any reduction in endurance or changes in handling characteristics. Maximum speed is 414 m.p.h., and maximum range, with tip tanks, 570 n.m. Introduction of the Mk 4 into RAF service will mark a change in syllabus.'

Flight International, 31 August 1961 p.299.

That change to the syllabus was significant. Pilot training at the time of the introduction of the T.Mk.3 had been developed around 230 hours of actual flying time. Only 120 hours were currently spent on the Jet Provost itself, the rest were made up on the advanced jet training fleet, at that time comprising the Vampire 11 but soon to be superseded by the Folland Gnat. With the introduction of the higher performance T.Mk.4, it was now possible to retain the student within the training establishment for longer, moving a proportion of the fast jet syllabus onto the FTS. In fact, only seventy hours were required on 'operational trainers' due to the inclusion of the T.Mk.4, constituting a significant saving in the training of pilots.

DEVELOPMENT

What many consider the ultimate 'sporty' Jet Provost had a typical Hunting pedigree. The T.Mk.4, T.Mk.5 & BAC-167 Strikemaster can be traced back to a development programme for the Jindivik. As noted in the preceding chapters, trials on the up-rated Viper 11 had begun in mid-June 1957, when G-AOUS, the company technology demonstrator, was modified to take the more powerful engine. In 1958, along with two T.Mk.3s modified on the production line to T.Mk.4 standard, G-AOUS undertook trials for the proposed T.4 production run. In September 1959 the modified T.Mk.2 performed at Farnborough, pressing home the increased 2,500lbs= thrust performance of the Viper 11. The first mock-up T.Mk.4, XN467, flew on 15 July 1960. Interestingly, the aircraft was now a BAC product, the corporation having been officially launched two weeks previously.

Tragedy struck the programme on 16 November 1960, when G-AOUS, piloted by Lt Cdr J.R.S. Overbury, a Hunting test pilot since 1957, took off from Luton on airspeed trials. The aircraft was recovering from a dive at the maximum design speed, when the positive G encountered forced the nose leg to descend into the airflow. The leg and both nose undercarriage doors were promptly ripped off, forcing the aircraft to violently pitch, nose upward. The rapid change in attitude caused both wings to detach and the fuselage to break-up. The pilot was killed. An obituary appeared in *Flight* on 25 November 1960.

Jack Overbury

It is with regret that we record that Lt Cdr J. R. S. Overbury lost his life on Wednesday of last week in an accident to a Jet Provost which he was test flying. Jack Overbury joined Hunting Aircraft from Saunders Roe Ltd, where as chief test pilot he had concluded the SR.53 prototype trials, in March last year. In 1954 he was awarded the de Havilland Trophy for a point-to-point London - Amsterdam record (at 571.5 m.p.h.) he set up in a Sea Hawk; and in 1955 he established a Rome - Malta record in a Sea Venom at a speed of 538 m.p.h. He had a serious accident at Sandown, IoW, in 1958 while demonstrating a Druine Turbulent. His injuries necessitated four operations and he was grounded for several months, only his determination to fly again bringing him back into the test pilot's profession.

Just a few weeks later on 2 December 1960, XN468, the second T.Mk.4 mock-up, was delivered from manufacture to Bristol Siddeley Engines Ltd at Filton. The aircraft flew a total of 68hr 55min, undertaking a series of assessment handling checks to test the Viper 11/Jet Provost combination before returning to Hunting Aircraft Ltd on 28 March 1961. The test programme did not go well. Flying was delayed for fourteen days due to bad weather; then the engine did not run smoothly, often 'kicking' into life towards the top end RPM. The entire throttle system had been incorrectly set up before the aircraft had been delivered, necessitating re-rigging and time-consuming engine runs. Then specially fitted monitoring test equipment was discovered to be '– *entirely unsatisfactory*', cracks appeared in some of the airframe equipment mounting brackets, and other venturi-based equipment proved impossible to calibrate. The culprit turned out to be a 10ft length of P4 instrumentation piping, found to be porous. The Jet Pipe Temperature (JPT) limiter amplifier refused to clear a fault, even when it itself was replaced and just when the team thought they were in the clear and the aircraft finally got into the air, the engine shed a turbine blade. By the time the aircraft was fully serviceable, it was time to hand the aircraft back to Huntings. Surprisingly, the tests were heralded a success with only one recommendation: the JPT gauge position was poor and needed to be re-sited.

The first production T.Mk.4 was delivered to Central Flying School, RAF Little Rissington.

Little else was modified on the T.Mk.4, save engine mounts and the length of the Refrasil blanket around the jet pipe. The improved performance won over the RAF, which placed an order with BAC for a further production run of 185 T.Mk.4s. The introduction of the Viper 11 (renamed the Viper 102 once in production) radically increased the potential of the aircraft. The static thrust at sea level alone was 2450lb; the Viper 8 (Viper 102) powered the T.Mk.3 at 1750lb, giving a permissible speed advantage of 50 knots. The T.Mk.4 could reach a sustained 35,000 + ft., 5,000ft more than its predecessor; however, this extra performance made for less effective fuel efficiency and thus reduced the range somewhat. The first production aircraft, XP547, flew on 4 August 1961 from what was by then known as the British Aircraft Corporation – Luton Division. XP547 was subsequently delivered to Boscombe Down for Qualitative Preview Handling Assessment (QPHA) and Certificate of Airworthiness prior to release to service. A further ten T.Mk.4s had made their way from Luton to Boscombe Down and Little Rissington by Christmas 1961.

The enhanced performance of the T.Mk.4 was only curtailed by the lack of cockpit pressurisation, and it wasn't long before BAC was proposing a pressurised version of the type. By the early 1960s the RAF also considered 'altitude' a tactical advantage, and so the Ministry of Aviation sponsored the British Aircraft Corporation to develop the next, and final, generation of Jet Provost.

BAC-145, 164, 166 & 167

On 16 March 1965 a T.Mk.4 (XS231) made the first of three proving flights. What made this aircraft (project code BAC-166) special was the introduction of the Viper

On 16 March 1965 a T.Mk.4, XS231, made the first of three proving flights. Project code BAC-166 introduced the Viper 522, offering an extra 1,000lb static thrust over the current T.Mk.4 powerplant. (British Aircraft Corporation)

522, offering an extra 1,000lb static thrust more than the current T.Mk.4 powerplant. XS231 was intended to be the test-bed for a range of new COIN developments designated BAC-164 (unpressurised) and BAC-167 (pressurised). The project was run in tandem with a Ministry of Aviation contract to develop and produce 110 T.Mk.5, pressurised cockpit aircraft for the Royal Air Force. Naturally, BAC capitalised on the Government sponsored programme, even operating one of the BAC-145s with an up-rated Viper-20 to a height of 40,000ft. The Jet Provost product range appeared to have no limitations; further contracts from the Government and the prospect of orders from abroad ensured the Luton workforce were kept to full capacity. From 1963 the factory had also been producing wing torsion boxes for the BAC 1-11, again an aircraft building a comprehensive order book. Moreover, Luton engineers were involved in a number of Ministry sponsored research programmes.

In 1959 Hunting Ltd had been awarded a contract, No.KD/23/01/CB10 (e), to build two research aircraft. Both were intended to provide figures relating to 'jet flap' operation, a form of VSTOL. The aircraft was constructed at Luton against Ministry of Aviation specification E.R.189D, and on 26 March 1963 the first airframe, XN714, flew at RAE Bedford, piloted by S.B. Oliver. This event was recorded by *Flight International*, and gives an insight into the handling characteristics of the aircraft.

'On the afternoon of March 26 Mr Oliver found everything, including the weather, to his liking. With flaps at ° he took the H.126 off at about 80Kt after a runoff some 600yd. Afterwards he said. "Taking this plane off is an entirely new sensation: it just floats off

The H.126, a ministry sponsored Hunting Percival-built aircraft on 'very' short finals at RAE Bedford.

the ground, and then you go up like a lift." He cruised around in a characteristic slightly nose-down attitude for some 18min, accompanied by a two-seat Meteor chase plane.'

Flight International, 4 April 1963, pp.454-455.

As the aircraft was purely research orientated it carried the minimum of systems, and in true Percival spirit existing technology was, where possible, reused. Consequently, the fuselage was a reworked Jet Provost airframe and the cockpit, now carrying one pilot, utilised a modified Mk.3 canopy. Interestingly, the aircraft had a nose mounted Bristol-Siddeley Orpheus engine, fed by a large central intake, not unlike one of the proposed arrangements offered by Hunting engineers during the early design phase of the P.84. The basic premise involved passing hot gases from the jet pipe over the upper surfaces of the flaps and ailerons, thus reducing take-off and landing speeds. During testing the aircraft routinely achieved a take-off speed of 35-40kt. The project was cancelled in 1968.

Detail work was also undertaken for a number of projects, including some weapon system components for other BAC manufacturers. Unfortunately, this was to be short lived. English Electric had two Guided Weapons factories, Luton and Stevenage, both employed in the manufacture of Thunderbird anti-aircraft missiles for the British Army. The company, at the time of its amalgamation into BAC, was also working on Blue Water and PT428. Blue Water, a tactical ground-to-ground nuclear weapon, internationally recognised as a world beater, was cancelled in 1962. The Luton wing of Guided Weapons closed soon after, with the loss of 1,000 jobs. PT428 was a different story. Designed as a low-level anti-aircraft platform, the contract was again cancelled in 1962. However, two years later the concept was resurrected under a project entitled ET316. This time the project prevailed and went on to become the Rapier, still in production today and with a worldwide order book. Both initial cancellations had been at the request of the Ministry of Defence, which wanted to maintain spending on the 'Mobile Air Force Project'. Unfortunately, these were the tip of the iceberg and when the Wilson-led Labour Government took power in October 1964, further defence cuts were its top priority.

Luton Closes

Central to the formation of the British Aircraft Corporation was the Tactical, Strike and Reconnaissance project - TSR2. The aircraft and its demise has been much published and do not require further explanation here; however, the effect it had on the British aerospace industry and particularly Luton is important to our story. TSR2 and other supporting aircraft projects, namely the VSTOL P1154 and HS681 transport, had been the constant focus of attacks by the Labour Party whilst in opposition. Moreover the fact that costs continued spiralling unchecked placed them squarely in the firing line. The premise was simple: why continue to develop three technologically advanced aircraft at a cost so far unknown but likely to be over £750 million for TSR2 alone, when machines from America could be purchased at a fraction of that. The incoming Labour Cabinet, mindful of public opinion, set about discussing the future of a number of aviation projects within weeks of entering office.

On 26 October 1964 the newly elected Labour Government issued a statement on the worsening economic 'situation' now gripping the United Kingdom. Included within the proposed measures was *'particular emphasis'* on scrapping *'prestige'* projects. Along with the three military aircraft under consideration was one civil project – Concorde. Luckily for BAC, Concord was not a solely British venture and had been the subject of a binding International Treaty with France. The Wilson administration soon discovered that to cancel the UK's obligations would be impossible. Roy Jenkins, Minister of Aviation, discussed the possibility with French Ministers in November 1964. The three-day session did not go well. As the aircraft was bound by international law, the French would hear nothing of abandoning the project. Rumours in the French press circulated the idea that the Americans were behind Britain's reasons for wanting to pull out, clearly with the aim of destroying the French aviation industry. By the end of the year Jenkins had been left in no doubt as to where the UK stood. If they did, indeed, pull out, the French Government would seek compensation through the Hague; to make matters worse it was clear the British would lose. The implications of withdrawal would have far-reaching consequences, not least still having to fund half the project through compensation whilst not benefiting from any subsequent research information. The Government had no option but to proceed. TSR2's fate was now sealed and with it the future of the Luton plant.

The cancellation of TSR2 had severe implications for the BAC workforce. An estimated 5,000 lost their jobs in BAC alone, whilst union figures suggested another 3-4,000 were affected across supply and component firms. BAC, the company formed to build such technologically advanced aircraft, was now in a precarious position. The systematic reduction of military projects appeared to many outside the Government to be unsustainable, and consequently financial backers began to question their security. It was also clear that a reduction in labour would not stave off the crisis, leaving the BAC Board with no option but to rearrange production on existing contracts, and inevitably, consider site closure. When the decision came it was a complete surprise. Luton was to close, with all current work distributed to other sites. Luton, thanks mainly to the efforts of Arthur Summers, Managing Director of Hunting Aircraft, had become a model of aircraft production; however, it was size that counted. The site was to be stripped of the Jet Provost, sending wing construction to Hurn and everything else to Preston. To many, this seemed the beginning of the end for BAC: in moving

An artist's impression of the proposed Mk.5. (British Aircraft Corporation)

In the days before computer design the artist sometimes struggled (compare with photo above). The idea here is to indicate versatility. (British Aircraft Corporation)

work from Luton the Board had dramatically increased production costs. Other contracts were in the pipeline, as this extract from Hansard clearly demonstrates, but how secure they were was a matter of speculation:

'396
Sir Ian Orr-Ewing
asked the Minister of Aviation what production orders he has placed for the maritime version of the Comet; and for how many.

Mr. Hastings
asked the Minister of Aviation when he expects to place a firm order for the Maritime Comet, the P1127 and the Anglo-French Jaguar.

Mr. Roy Jenkins
The order for the Maritime Comet should be placed shortly subject to the successful completion of contract negotiations for full development and production. It is not the practice to disclose the size of military orders.

On the P1127, I have nothing to add to the reply given by my right hon. Friend the Secretary of State for Defence on 24th November. Preliminary work on the Anglo-French Jaguar is going ahead well, but we have not yet reached a stage when firm production orders can be placed.

Sir Ian Orr-Ewing
Will the Minister press on with the orders? He will know that the British aircraft industry is in a parlous position and that this very day there has been an announcement that B.A.C. is to close its factory at Luton, causing about 1,850 employees to be thrown out of work. Does not the right hon. Gentleman realise that it is most important that these aircraft orders should be placed at the earliest possible date?

Mr. Jenkins
It is important that firm orders should be placed when we have arrived at the right stage, but not before. The hon. Gentleman will be aware that the numbers employed in the industry are still greatly in excess of those which were expected to be employed when the cancellation of the TSR2 was made.

Mr. R. Carr
Will the right hon. Gentleman bear in mind that these production orders are vital to the aircraft industry and that the Government will have had getting on for the best part of a year now to come to a conclusion?

Mr. Jenkins
That does not mean that a great deal of work has not been done on the P1127. A great deal is being done.

House of Commons Debate, 8 December 1965, vol. 722 c396.

Eight days later the closure was communicated to the aviation community by a press release in *Flight International*. As the industry eagerly awaited the publication of the Plowden Report, a far-reaching enquiry on the future of the industry, the sense of irony was clearly apparent.

'BAC Luton to Close

The Luton factory of British Aircraft Corporation is to be closed in July 1966. Announcing this on December 8 the company stated: "BAC announces with regret that, as part of the reorganisation following the TSR.2 cancellation and inline with the national policy to reduce the size of the aircraft industry, they cannot continue to employ the present labour force and fully use the existing facilities of the group. They have therefore no alternative but to close the Luton factory, a decision which has been taken with great reluctance in view of the fine record of the factory. . . ."

Possibilities of alternative employment were being explored by the company, the statement added, "and a number of employees will be interviewed and offered situations in other divisions of the corporation. "Vauxhall Motors would acquire the factory premises and offer jobs to many BAC employees, and English Electric would also be offering employment.'

Flight International, 16 December 1965 p. 1,028

T.Mk.5

On 28 February 1967 XS230, a hybrid version of the T.Mk.4, flew from Warton for the first time. Both this aircraft and the BAC-166 programme had been delayed whilst the partially constructed airframes were taken, as Luton closed, to Warton by road. The combination of the more powerful Viper 201 and pressurised cockpit area made the aircraft a very attractive proposition for many limited-budget air forces. Consequently the BAC-145, destined for the RAF, was further developed, eventually spawning twelve variants as the BAC-167 – the Strikemaster (discussed in the following chapter). The proposed unpressurised BAC-164 COIN development was killed off whilst still on the drawing board. On 14 January 1969 the RAF eventually ordered 110 T.Mk.5s. The type became a familiar sight across the training units, occasionally necessitating modification for specialist operations. XW287, the first true production model, arrived at CFS HQ at Little Rissington on 3 September 1969, just under three years after the first flight.

Testing Times

The BAC-145 was a sound enough proposition. Capitalising on the powerful Viper 201 engine's ability to provide nearly 1,000lb more thrust, the aircraft combined the power of the T.Mk.4 with increased, sustainable altitude. Again initial work was by private venture; however, BAC already had a full suit of figures produced through the T.Mk.4 programme. The Ministry of Aviation placed an initial contract for the development of the T.Mk.5 airframe in the winter of 1964; however, by then work was already at an advanced stage. Funding did allow further work to be carried out between mid-1965 and 1966 at the Royal Aircraft Establishment's transonic wind tunnel facility at Farnborough. A 1/12th-scale model of the aircraft, sting mounted and carrying four loaded stores pylons was tested over a mach number rage of .30 to .83 for the flight range of incidence and sideslip.

The most noticeable change to the airframe arrangement was the redesigned front end. To withstand a crew-pressurised environment, a major rebuild of the frontal area forward of the main spar was required. Just as the Percival engineers had done fifteen years previously, a new cockpit area, retaining very little of the original, was fitted to the airframe. The BAC team conducted a number of initial handling and

Wind tunnel tests allowed the manufacturer to look forward to the Strikemaster and its payload. This is a twelfth scale model at RAE Bedford.

performance checks to ensure the redesigned shape was, as wind tunnel tests had suggested, airworthy; unfortunately it was not. During the stall test phase Warton engineers noted:

> 'The stalling behaviour in the initial build configuration was considered unsatisfactory. The stalling speeds were high and the stall itself was indeterminate – there being no nose warning drop in any configuration. However, stall warning, similar to the Mk.4., was present in the form of light airframe buffet.'

First Prototype Jet Provost T.Mk.5 XS230. Despatch Brochure for A&AEE Boscombe Down. Flight Test Report AFN/JP/8

Alarmed at the unruly characteristics, BAC allowed A&AEE pilots to fly an initial preview test from Warton for a second opinion. They confirmed the initial finding, and filed a further report regarding the oscillatory nature of the spin. A series of extra spinning tests using different fuel configurations and the re-rigging of elevator deflections had little effect on the phenomenon. Consequently a series of structural modifications were incorporated; all can still be recognised on the T.Mk.5.

> '4.1 Stalling Tests

> 'A more detailed investigation was then carried out on the 2nd prototype Mk.5 (XS231) and also a Mk.4 aircraft (XR669) to establish the causes of the differences in stalling characteristics between the two marks.

XS231 had, in true Percival tradition, a hand built pressurised cockpit fitted after the project was moved to the Warton complex. (British Aircraft Corporation)

'- about this time it was found from tests on another Jet Provost variant, that a small leading edge slat at the wing root also gave satisfactory stalling behaviour and, as this change was simple to incorporate, this solution was therefore adopted.

'These small root slats (4" span) were fitted to XS230 and the good CL max. and nose drop behaviour was confirmed; after fitting some fences beneath the air intakes the stall warning was also fully adequate.

'4.2 Spinning Tests

'Strakes (3" wide) were fitted to the nose extending longitudinally over the length of the Rebecca aerial "housing". An improvement was immediately apparent so the strakes were increased in width to 4" and finally in a much strengthened form to 4.5 ins. In this final configuration, stable spins were being achieved from fuel states of 1,700lb. down to 500lb. Below this, some oscillation did occur, therefore a minimum fuel limit of 500lb. is proposed for all spinning. A&AEE pilots assessed the aircraft in this configuration and they also found the spinning characteristics satisfactory down to 500lb. fuel state.'

First Prototype Jet Provost T.Mk.5 XS230. Despatch Brochure for A&AEE Boscombe Down. Flight Test Report AFN/JP/8

The new cockpit provided a pressurised environment capable of withstanding a maximum differential pressure of +3.5psi in the event of a pressure controller failure. During normal operation, the pressure differential would be 3psi at 38,000ft. The canopy was also completely redesigned. Gone was the 'handraulic' winding handle;

The locations of the spinning and stalling modifications required to make the T.Mk.5 safe.

now the canopy was powered up and down a fixed rail at the press of a button, allowing the cockpit to be better sealed when closed. XS230 had no facility for canopy jettison; however, the intention was to ensure the system was operational on subsequent models. The cockpit was pressurised by tapping air from the final stage of the engine compressor and then passing it through a refrigeration unit and on into the cockpit area. The tap-off also provided windscreen de-mist and pressure for the canopy seal. A new demand oxygen system, supplied from three 750ltr cylinders housed in the new nose section, ensured the crew could safely operate at the increased altitude.

Two further fuel tanks, one in each wing, enhanced the capacity by 650lb, substantially compensating for the increased weight of the cockpit modifications. The tanks differed in that they were 'integral', basically a void in the wings was sealed and filled, rather than bag tanks as fitted to previous marks. The facility for tip tanks was retained; however, only a few RAF aircraft, predominantly those required for navigation training at No.6 FTS RAF Finningley, were fitted. Interestingly, those aircraft with tip tanks did not require the nose strakes, as the tanks were just as effective at keeping the aircraft stable about the normal axis. The Royal Air Force committed to the aircraft on 14 January 1969.

'RAF Jet Provost Order

'A contract for the supply of more than 100 new Jet Provost Mk 5 basic trainers for the Royal Air Force, placed by MinTech on behalf of the MoD, was announced by British Aircraft Corporation on Tuesday of last week, January 14 (Flight, Sensor, January 16). Describing the order, BAC said, "This follows the decision to replace the existing Mk 4

Jet Provost announced in the 1967 Defence Estimates. It supersedes the present interim arrangements and marks the successful conclusion of formal contractual negotiations. The Jet Provost Mk 5 is identical, save for the engine, to the BAC 167 Strikemaster, which has so far attracted export orders for 76 aircraft, worth £12.5 million. The addition of over 100 aircraft to BAC Preston Division's production line at Warton will mean a powerful sales boost to the Strikemaster in which a number of countries are known to be interested."'

Flight International, 23 January 1969, p. 145.

As the aircraft went into production, work was continuing on improvements to the canopy aspects of the escape system. The aircraft was fitted with an assisted escape system as standard; however, the redesigned cockpit had necessitated a new canopy. The early model T.Mk.5s all had a canopy jettison facility, which, due to the nature of the new structure, added precious time to the ejection sequence. The jettison system on the T.Mk.3 was a simple affair; in the event of either seat being initiated, the canopy was jettisoned first.

'5. When the firing unit sear is removed, the cartridge is fired and gas pressure, operating a shuttle valve is directed to both jettison jacks. Initial jack movement unlocks the canopy rail locking hooks and subsequent movement lifts the canopy and rails clear of the airframe assisted by airflow.'

AP 101B-2303A-15 Page 1 (AL6)

There was also the facility for jettison independent of seat firing. In normal operation the canopy was closed manually via a winding handle, to open one simply disengaged this mechanism and slid the canopy back.

The redesigned T.Mk.5 frontal area made this process impossible. Initially, the canopy was to be jettisoned in a similar way to the earlier system; however, this proved to be problematic. Not least in the spin, when it was discovered during jettison trials on XS231 that there was '- *an unacceptably long time delay between canopy jettison and ejection seat initiation to ensure that there was no interference between the jettisoned canopy and the seat system.*' The answer lay in a new system – Miniature Detonating Cord (MDC). As the first aircraft were appearing at their units, the RAF, armed with new figures from BAC's test programme, requested the use of MDC as the primary method of clearing the ejection path. A number of proving trials were undertaken at A&AEE utilising the blower tunnel facility between December 1971 and July 1972, with the result that MDC became a standard requirement for the T.Mk.5. Now in an emergency:

'4. The canopy disintegration system incorporates two cartridge firing units, one at the rear of each ejection seat, a sheathed MDC bonded to the inner surface of the transparency and a detonator assembly. Each cartridge is fired by withdrawal of its firing pin sear and a safety pin is provided for each sear.

'6. When the firing sear is withdrawn, the cartridge is fired and the gas pressure is directed via the shuttle valve to the detonator block on the canopy frame. A striker pin is opened to detonate the MDC and the canopy disintegrates on the frame.

AP 101B-2305-15 Page 2

MDC pattern on test aircraft at Boscombe Down, note two dummy pilots helmets. (AEN/65/025(A) 24 May 1973)

The introduction of this system reduced the time needed between canopy clearance and the seats leaving the aircraft; however, it presented its own unique hazard. The cord, 1.6mm in diameter, was contained within a 'D' shaped elastomer backing strip; on detonation, this tended to blast into the cockpit area. On the Boscombe trials this had caused facial damage to test dummies. The majority of the debris entering the cockpit was negated by fitting a stainless steel shield around the MDC at the extremities of the cockpit Perspex. However, it could not be fitted around the central areas without limiting visibility, and to prevent splatter from this a neck shield was incorporated into the aircrew helmet. The T.Mk.5 canopy structure differed in one respect from its earlier variant, it had no central stiffening member as the acrylic sheet was more substantial. In August 1971, the RAF requested a study into the value of fitting MDC to the T.Mk.3 & T.Mk.4. As a pre-requisite to trials with MDC, A&AEE recommended that through-canopy exit trials were needed in case of MDC malfunction. And so during November 1973 a Jet Provost was back in front of the Blower Tunnel at Boscombe Down. The results speak for themselves:

'5.1 IMPACTS On all tests the seat head box removed only a small area of transparency, with little or no forward extension. The dummy's head had then to force its own path clear resulting in neck loads higher than those recorded on unimpeded ejection tests; the highest loads were associated with Tests 1 and 3 in which the seat and dummy were ejected through a complete transparency.'

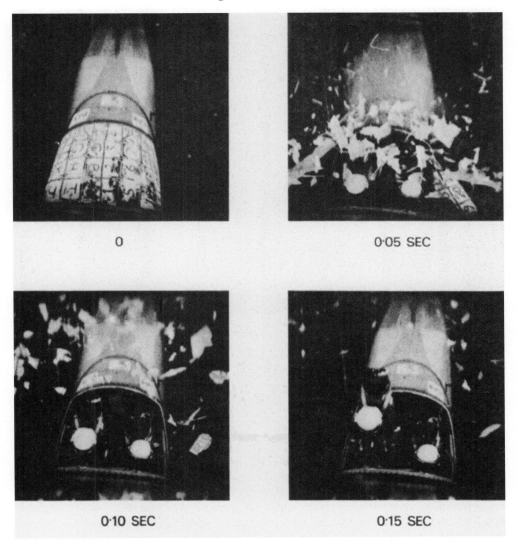

Canopy breakup at 90kt. Picture taken using a 16mm 2,000pps camera. (AEN/65/025(A) 24 May 1973)

Jet Provost MKS 3 and 4 - Ejection Through Canopy Trials. MOD Ref AH/661/047 13 November 1974.

The same could not be said for the proposed T.Mk.5:

'4.4 Test 4 – 90 KNOTS To assess the performance of the seat and canopy under the conditions of MDC failure, the seat and dummy were ejected through the canopy. The MDC was fitted to the transparency in the normal way.

'The starboard seat was ejected through the transparency with the overhead MDC pattern unfired, and although there were larger pieces of Perspex surrounding the dummy, by comparison with those obtained using MDC, it was considered very satisfactory.'

A test dummy plays the part of groundcrew during canopy disintegration trials. (AEN/65/025(A) 24 May 1973)

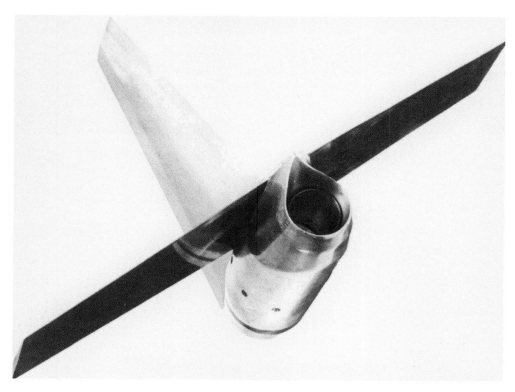

As late as 1979 attempts were being made to quieten down the T.Mk.5. This wind tunnel model was for the redesign of the nib. (National Gas Turbine Establishment)

Jet Provost MK 5 – Miniature Detonating Cord Clearance Trials. MOD Ref AH/563/02 24 May 1973

The final pure T.Mk.5 machine, XW437, was delivered on 6 October 1972 to RAF Cranwell; since retirement it has been in private ownership in the USA. Three days later, No.6 FTS RAF Finningley took XW438 on charge, a T.Mk.5B (Navigation Training) variant. The last deliveries of the MOD contract were not the end of the story – far from it. Building on previous exports of the T.51 and T.52, the BAC team were already chalking up sales of their ground strike and support trainer the BAC-167 Strikemaster. The aircraft was to take the Jet Provost story well into the twenty-first century. The role all three types played in flying training and the display teams they formed in the 1970s are the subject of the next chapter.

5.

'With Jet Provosts we are using up a tremendous lot of sky'

'The Jet Provost is an extremely docile aeroplane, yet it can give a lively aerobatic performance, as evidenced by the Central Flying School's outstanding exhibitions at Farnborough and other air displays. Because of this it can be used right from the ab initio stage up to the point where the student is a competent and confident light-jet pilot, ready in every way to go on to the advanced trainer. In this respect it is superior to the tail-down piston-engined Provost, the step from which to the Vampire Trainer was far greater than that from the Jet Provost, which has a power/weight ratio roughly similar to the Vampire's. The Jet Provost's spinning characteristics are good; its rate of roll is fast, and take-off and landing are extremely simple. Its engine-handling techniques are in line with those required by the more powerful jet engines and its response admirably prepares the student for the Vampire.'

Air Ministry Quote, July 1960.

By the early 1960s the majority of Flying Training Schools had re-equipped with, or were about to receive, Jet Provosts. Whilst the consequences of Duncan Sandys' 1957 Defence White Paper slowly affected other units, the Jet Provost was destined to become the champion of Cold War flying training. The schools and squadrons who operated the aircraft, the stations they called home and the flying teams they displayed at many airshows around the United Kingdom are the subject of this chapter.

CENTRAL FLYING SCHOOL

On 31 August 1959 the first batch of six T.Mk.3s arrived at the Central Flying School, RAF Little Rissington. Whereupon QFIs began the process of updating the course syllabus first cut with the three T.Mk.1s four years earlier. By November 1961 two T.Mk.4s had arrived. The station was built between 1936 and 1938 and was officially opened as an Aircraft Storage, and later Maintenance, Unit. At the time it was the highest airfield in the country at 750ft above sea level, causing many 'interesting' meteorological situations (see Roy Davey's account below). The station received its first runway in 1941½ as part of a major programme to surface all the ASUs in the Cotswold area. As well as storage and rectification duties, the station was home to No.6 FTS until the end of the war. Central Flying School was reformed in 1946 and moved from Hullavington to the Cotswold station that same year.

XM425 T3 delivered to CFS in March 1960 (Bigbird Aviation)

"My only brush with the JP3 was when I was on the staff at the Central Flying School in 1960/1 when we seemed to have a spate of incidents involving landing the JP short of the runway at the basic flying training schools (on one occasion with my two very senior officer bosses on board). Because I was involved in the flight safety aspect, as CFS was a sub-group headquarters and I was the jack-of-all-trades as secretary to the Commandant, it was suggested that I had a quick trip to familiarise myself with the problem. According to my logbook I flew with a Flt Lt Beck on 26th June 1961. I remember some aspects of that trip, including the fact that it was under-powered and quite easy to drop in short of the runway if you let the speed drop on the final approach. Very easy to do at Little Rissington as it was on the top of a hill, had rubbish approaches (over valleys) and the runways were not that long!"

Roy Davey, QFI CFS Little Rissington.

CFS moved to RAF Cranwell from Little Rissington in 1976. The move was unpopular to many as it disjointed the school, the aircraft elements necessary for QFI training being spread across Leeming (Bulldog), Valley (Gnat) as well as Cranwell (Jet Provost and Ground School). Flying within the QFI course required eighty-five hours on the Jet Provost including twenty hours conversion to type and twenty-eight hours Basic Instructional Phase, both on the T.Mk.3A. The subsequent Advanced Phase covered a further thirty-eight hours, this time on the T.Mk.5A. In just over a year CFS HQ moved to Leeming, where it remained with the Jet Provost element until the station closed in advance of regeneration for Tornado in mid-1984. CFS was then housed with the remnants of the No.3 FTS fleet (16 A/C) at Scampton until its closure 31 May 1995, whereupon CFS and No.3 FTS merged on moving back to Cranwell.

No.1 Flying Training School.

No.1 FTS arrived at Linton-on-Ouse on 18 November 1958, operating Piston Provosts for the training of Fleet Air Arm personnel. On 19 August 1960 the first T.Mk.3

Oxygen charging on the line at RAF Little Rissington in the early 1960s

Refuelling XN584, a T.Mk.3 at Little Rissington.

XW289 T5A, based at RAF Linton-on-Ouse, one of the last aircraft to be demobbed in 1993 (Bigbird Aviation)

arrived at the Yorkshire station, followed two years later (27 April 1962) by the first T.Mk.4. RAF Linton-on-Ouse was originally built as a bomber station, and formed part of the Scheme 'J' expansion programme, opening on 13 May 1937. Aircraft from the station were involved in early leaflet raids and the first 1,000 bomber formation to Cologne. From 1943 the station played host to squadrons of 6 Group Royal Canadian Air Force until, towards the end of the war, it transferred to Transport Command involved in the repatriation of POWs. However, Linton-on-Ouse moved back onto the front line when Fighter Command arrived, along with a detachment of Sector Headquarters staff, a situation that remained until the station closed in early 1957. This turned out to be a temporary measure, as by September the station had reopened to accept No.1 FTS operating Piston Provosts from Syerston.

From 1969 Linton-on-Ouse exclusively trained Royal Air Force pilots to Wings Standard, prior to selection for Fast Jet, Helicopter or Multi-Engine aircraft. The increased unit task necessitated taking on Topcliffe as a Relief Landing Ground (RLG) in 1974, and Dishforth was later transferred to Linton-on-Ouse in 1983 in advance of the closure of Leeming. By 1985 Airwork Ltd was undertaking some support work on station, including engineering tasks on the Jet Provosts. The last course to train on the JP graduated on 4 July 1993, by then No.1 FTS had amassed over 600,000 on the type.

No.2 Flying Training School.

In November 1957 No.2 Flying Training School, which had pioneered the '*all-through jet training*' concept at Hullavington, was earmarked to receive the first of the new T.Mk.3s. The school was, by then, stationed at RAF Syerston; the first aircraft arrived on 26 June 1959. The initial course started in October that year, graduating the following June 1960. The introduction of the Jet Provost demonstrated a time saving of six weeks on the existing scheme. A number of other time-saving innovations were also introduced. Now all training up to Wings level would be undertaken at one station and under one commandant. Prior to the Jet Provost, the student spent nine months at one station and a further nine months at a different station. The training delivery also received a review. From the introduction of the Jet Provost each student would, where possible, be the responsibility of one instructor. Previously instruction was ad hoc, relying more on who was available at the time. Naturally this did not help the assessment process, single tutor profiles allowed the weak student to be identified earlier and so had a cost-saving implication. Wings were achieved within a year having had 160 hours on type.

RAF Syerston transferred to flying training in February 1948. When No.22 Flying Training School arrived, specialising in pilots for the Fleet Air Arm, Percival Prentice and Provost aircraft were tasked with the role. On 1 May 1955 the school was reformed as No.1 FTS, but continued its FAA commitment at Syerston until November 1957, when the school was redeployed to RAF Linton-on-Ouse. Confusingly, the school was replaced by No.2 FTS, who reformed at the station on 18 November 1957. For the next ten years the station was home to No.2 FTS, until a downturn in the number of pilots required forced a re-assessment of flying training and the school was disbanded on 16 January 1970 as part of defence cuts.

No.3 Flying Training School.

RAF Leeming was one of seventeen stations of Standard Function to be started in 1939; by 1943 it formed part of 6 Group RCAF along with many other stations in

XW431 T.Mk5A, Based at RAF Leeming throughout the 1970s – early 1980s. Note the CFS badge and 'trolley acc' to right of photo.

the North Yorkshire area. After the war, the station played host to a number of night fighter squadrons operating Mosquitoes, Meteors and Javelins, before being handed over to flying training. No.3 Flying Training School was reformed at Leeming in September 1961, as a new Jet Provost training unit, the T.Mk.4, was also at the station throughout the 1960s. A Relief Landing Ground was designated at RAF Dishforth; however, Topcliffe was also used on occasion. In December 1973 the Refresher Flying School moved to the station from Manby, but by 1977 it had become Refresher Flying Squadron. No.3 FTS was disbanded on 24 April 1984, when the station was closed whilst the site was prepared for the F3 Tornado. No.3 FTS, somewhat mauled by the ravages of defence cuts, currently survives at RAF Cranwell. Central Flying School HQ was a lodger unit at Leeming from September 1977 until the station's closure; by a strange quirk of fate it now forms part of 3 FTS at Cranwell.

ROYAL AIR FORCE COLLEGE CRANWELL

The Jet Provost made its first appearance at the Royal Air Force College Cranwell in June 1960, when XM451 was delivered to the airfield; T.Mk.3 and T.Mk.3A were operated by the college until November 1979. T.Mk.4s complimented the training effort for ten years between 1961 and 1971. The replacement of the T.Mk.4 started in 1970, and the first T.Mk.5s appeared in December that year. Over the period all marks operated at the College, they amassed an incredible 563,000 hours on type.

This vast amount of hours in such a short space of time was typical of training aircraft; further, the hours are not all spent in straight and level flight. On specific sections of flying training courses the aircraft could be flying 'rollers' or 'touch and goes' for days at a time. As one would expect, this took its toll on both undercarriage and tyres, whilst heavy or sustained braking consumed a vast amount of brake units. Each unit had its own section that repaired the wheels, tyres and brakes. Ed Austin, the Airframes Sergeant in charge of the Wheel and Hydraulic Workshops at RAF Cranwell, supported an incredible eighty-four T.Mk.3s and 4s from mid-1966 to mid-1969. Interestingly, the different marks brought with them a range of problems:

"The JP3 could hold the aircraft stationary with the handbrake on, with the engine at full power. The JP4 had more engine power, but the same brake units, which could not handle the extra power, so they slipped and quickly overheated. If one brake unit had new pads, and the other had bedded-in pads, the aircraft wouldn't stay in a straight line when braking."

The age-old problem with the undercarriage retraction system, a situation you will recall that caused major headaches for the Treasure, was becoming ever more apparent, as Sgt Austin describes:

"The JP had just one hydraulic actuator that through pulleys, bell-cranks, universal joints, and cables, hauled the three undercarriage units and doors up and down. The manufacturer didn't put bushes and an adequate lubrication system in the universal joints, so it wasn't long before the bush-less bearing holes all wore out, causing lost motion and adjustment problems. We were issued with the modification kits, and told to get on with it. Drill swarf all over our pristine hydraulic benches was now acceptable! We had no drill presses, so vices and hand drills were used. The unusual drill sizes had to be specially ordered. Adjustable reamers were required to achieve the optimum hole and bush dimensions. There were no spare units, so each aircraft was grounded until we completed a set. On the first set, we got the dozens of holes drilled and reamed, and the bushes fitted,

XP566 & XP582 T.Mk.4s based at RAF Cranwell buzz College Hall in the early 1960s. (courtesy MOD)

but the plated bolts wouldn't go in the bushes. Do we over-bore the bushes, or do we ask the vendor to supply us with thinner bolts? We went for option three. We were ordered to sandpaper the bolts until they fitted. The entire fleet was done like that!"

Other attributes of the aircraft systems pneumatic origins were still in evidence almost ten years later. Quite a number still had to be shaken out of the maintenance programme, Whilst others, when fixed, continued to remain within the Air Publication and be called up as an 'Out of Phase' check, wasting valuable hours on the ground:

"The Dunlop Hydraulic Brake Control Valve had a low pressure leak test after servicing. The test had been done and certified for many years in accordance with the Dunlop Manual. I found that we couldn't do the test because we couldn't find a hydraulic pressure gauge that was calibrated to such low pressures. Dunlop wrestled with the problem for several months, then removed the test from their manuals. They couldn't explain how the test ever got into the Manuals in the first place, but I suspect that they had originally based the test on that for their Pneumatic Brake Control Valves.

"The JP nose undercarriage had a 'liquid spring' shock absorber. It was made from thick, heavy steel to withstand enormous pressures. It worked very well, though it required careful servicing with 'special oil' that came in tiny containers, and smelled like hair oil. The trick was not to allow any air into the cylinder.

"The nosewheel castored on a self-centring cam. The cam, the cam fastener, bush and roller took turns at breaking or cracking, which required the assembly to be called off for

Strapping in a foreign student in the 1960s at Cranwell.

checks at regular intervals. Eventually, all the parts were strengthened and modified, so there was no further problems, but the RAF insisted on removing the nose undercarriage for many years afterwards."

Sgt Ed Austin, RAF Cranwell 1966-1969.

A number of aircraft became the 'station hack' or were loaned to other squadrons and stations supposedly for essential or spin experience flying. However not everybody looked after the aircraft like they should.

"One day, a set of wheels and brake units came into the workshop in a very sorry state. They looked as though they had been in an aircraft fire, we'd never seen anything like it. The reason became apparent when we learned that they had come off an aircraft that had been loaned to Coningsby where the pilots who were waiting for their Phantom's to arrive, wanted something to play with. They were used to landing with the brakes full on. The JP's didn't have an anti-skid system!"

GOLDEN EAGLE FLIGHT

Cranwell and the Jet Provost enjoyed royal patronage when on 20 August 1971 Flight Lieutenant The Prince of Wales received his flying badge from the then Chief of Air Staff, Air Chief Marshal Sir Denis Spotswood. The Prince had earlier gained a Private Pilot's Licence on the Chipmunk before gaining his instrument rating on the Bassett CC.1. He then moved to RAFC Cranwell where, between 8 March and 30 July

XW408 T.Mk.5A. Taken in 1989 in similar pose to the previous shot, note the 'Cranwell sash', a light blue tailband. (courtesy MOD)

1971 he flew T,Mk.5s. Two brand new aircraft XW322 & XW323 were formed into what became known as 'Golden Eagle Flight', having specific instructors and ground crew where possible. The Viper engine was brought up to the highest modification state available to ensure peak performance. The two aircraft both survive, XW322 as a flying example in the USA and XW323 as an exhibit at the RAF Museum Hendon.

No.6 Flying Training School.

No.6 Flying Training School was reformed at Little Rissington after the war, moving swiftly to Ternhill at the end of April 1946. By 1953 the unit's primary aircraft was the Percival Provost. The school moved again in July 1961, this time across the Pennines to RAF Acklington, Northumberland, and converted to the Jet Provost. RAF Acklington was an expansion period airfield constructed in 1938. Aviation was not new to the site: it had previously formed part of the First World War Home Defence network against Zeppelin raids down Britain's East Coast and the industrial areas of the North-East. During the Battle of Britain, the station housed a Sector Operations Room and four fighter squadrons as part of 13 Group. The first T.Mk.3 Jet Provosts had arrived by late 1961 and within eighteen months these had been complimented by the delivery of the T.Mk.4s.

Aircraft Electrician John Moran had been stationed at Acklington for just four months and was working the flight line when tragedy struck:

"The aircraft were practicing for the AOC's parade, all of the serviceable kites were on the flypast except one which was doing aerobatics. I was tasked with doing the turn-round on this particular aircraft and then starter crew. I went round the plane with the pilot as he did his pre-flight checks. I then strapped him in, plugged in his radio and removed the ejection pins and stored them. He started up and I marshalled him out and he was off. On one manoeuvre he did a loop and for some unknown reason he didn't get out of it and it was reported that the aircraft hit a tree stump and exploded, killing the pilot. It was very traumatic watching this and the activity immediately after it happened. The F700, which I had just signed, was whisked away from the line office. A court of enquiry and a court of inquest were convened and I had to attend both of them to answer a load of questions. Before the court hearings happened, the line chief told me to take some leave and they would contact me when to come back. This was my first posting and I was very green behind the ears, he could obviously see that I was very badly shaken up. The result was put down as pilot error but one always wonders!"

The unit was disbanded on 30 June 1968. No.6 FTS later reformed at RAF Finningley in 1970. The task for the school was radically different from its former incarnation. Combining Nos. 1 & 2 Air Navigation School, operating Varsity and the Airman Aircrew Initial Training School, the station became the principle Navigation training station until the unit moved to Cranwell under 55 (Reserve) Squadron in November 1996. Finningley's Jet Provosts were the usual range of T.Mk.3s, 4s and 5s; however, the latter had some additions. The T.Mk.5b carried tip tanks for extra duration, ensuring a far better flying profile during the low-level navigation phase. The aircraft

XW352 T.Mk.5B 'Romeo' of No.6 FTS tip tanks were fitted for the navigation trainer role.

ALVIS LEONIDES

Chosen after competitive trials to power the Percival
P.56 "Provost" the new basic trainer for the Royal Air Force

ALVIS LIMITED · COVENTRY · ENGLAND

1 Alvis celebrates the union between their engine and the Percival Provost in 1951. (*The Aeroplane*)

2 A Sultanate of Oman Airforce T.52 Percival Provost.

3 G-AOBU, Hunting Percival's T.Mk.1 company demonstrator. Note the company flash on the nose.

4 XD674 T.Mk.1 (7570M), RAF Finningley, 1970. This historic aircraft escaped a scrap notice and a trip to the fire dump! It now resides in the National Cold War Collection at Cosford.

5 A rare colour shot of G-AOUS. The T.Mk.2 broke up in November 1960, whilst recovering from a high speed dive.

6 Cranwell Poachers in original colours.

7 XN640 T.Mk.3 of Central Flying School, 1967. Delivered on 7 February 1962, this aircraft carries the typical Flying Training colour scheme of the '60s.

8 XR679 T.Mk.4 of No.1 Tactical Weapons Unit, 1983. TWU operated a small number of T.Mk.4s; this one sports an unusual camouflage paint scheme. (Pete James)

9 Jet Provost Trials Unit, Far East Air Force, 1965. Three aircraft were flown as part of a 'Forward Air Command' trial during the Indonesian Crisis. These two are parked next to the Fire Section at Butterworth. (Tam Mc Crorie)

10 Ejection Through Canopy Trials, A&AEE, 14 November 1973, utilising XP664, a redundant T.Mk.4 fuselage. (Courtesy MOD)

11 XS230 T.Mk.5P, Boscombe Down, 1988. This hybrid T.Mk.5P (the 'P' stands for prototype) was locally known as the T.Mk.4½. (Pete James)

12 A fine air-to-air shot of XS230. (Pete James)

13 XW429 T.Mk.5B 'Charlie', Finningley, 1990. No.6 Flying Training School used the T.Mk.5B for low-level navigation training; the tip tanks gave the aircraft a more usable duration.

14 XW302 T.Mk.5B 'Tango', Finningley, 1982, sporting the standard Flying Training colour scheme adopted by most units throughout the late 1970s-1980s.

15 XW301 T.Mk.5A fleet 63, Linton-on-Ouse. A standard appearance T.Mk.5A; note the unit identifier on the tail fairing and white rose station badge forward of the intake. (Pete James)

16 The Red Pelicans on the keys at Farnborough 1964. The Central Flying School team was eventually replaced by the Red Arrows as the RAF's primary display team.

17 Two Red Pelicans go over the top with smoke during a practice at RAF Little Rissington.

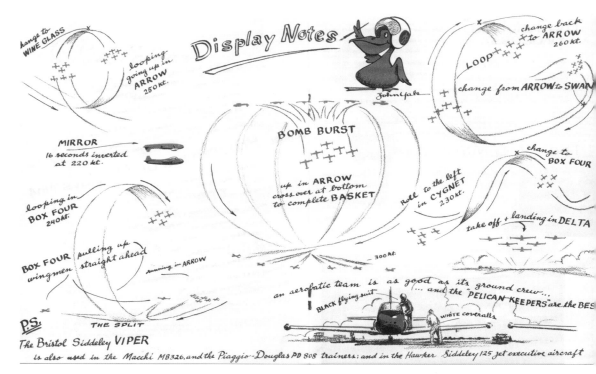

18 Centre-spread display note for the Red Pelicans' 1964 season.

19 A Kuwait Air Force T.51 in 'storage'. Note the reflective heat paint on the canopy and flat oleos!

20 Two T.Mk.3s of No.1 FTS at Boscombe Down, 1988. (Pete James)

21 Royal New Zealand Air Force Strikemaster Mk.88 lets loose with a salvo of Sura rockets. (RNZAF Official, via Air Force Museum, Christchurch, NZ)

22 The final ten Strikemasters on the assembly line at BAe Hurn, 1980. (Courtesy BAE Systems)

23 Ex-SOAF Strikemaster being prepared for delivery to the Singapore Air Force in 1977. Some aircraft changed hands many times.

24 Royal New Zealand Air Force Strikemaster Mk.88 and its replacement, the Australian-built Aermacchi MB339.
(RNZAF Official, via Air Force Museum, Christchurch, NZ)

25 XW374 T.Mk.5A of the Cranwell Poachers,1975.

26 XS217 T.Mk.4, RAF Halton, 1986. A large number of the high-fatigue T.Mk.4s made their way into ground-based training flights.

27 XM362 T.Mk.3, RAF Halton, 1986. This aircraft was used for training airframe technicians; it was moved to RAF Cosford in the early 1990s.

28 Privately owned T.Mk5s and T.Mk.3s are regular visitors to British and European air shows. These two are at Kemble, 2006.

29 Privately owned Strikemaster at Kemble, 2006.

30 A splendid shot from Kemble 2008, showing the clear linage between the Percival Provost P.56 and the BAC-145. (Picture by Adrian Pingstone)

were retired in 1993, Finningley was later closed under 'Front Line First' policy in 1996 and is now Robin Hood Airport.

No.7 Flying Training School.

Reformed at RAF Church Fenton, with the first T.Mk.3s arriving in March 1962, and T.Mk.4s mid 1963, No.7 FTS was disbanded on 30 November 1966 only to be reformed in 1979 at the same station. Mal Shaw worked on the line at Church Fenton until his fitters course in March 1965 and on return went into Rectification Flight before being posted onto 60 Sqd Javelins in Malaysia. While on rects, he came across the age-old problem of getting aircraft back on the line with limited spares and an overbearing SNCO.

"On Rectification Flt we would do, snags, Engine changes and routine servicing, Primary's Primary Star etc (from memory) I do remember there being a problem with the drive shaft from engine to accessory gear box (Hydraulic pumps, electric generator etc.) This drive shaft was "Chattering" for some reason and rapidly wearing the drive splines which we had to remove frequently and check for wear. One occasion (fresh from my "Fitters course") I wouldn't sign for a shaft because the splines were worn beyond limits and the Flt Sgt wasn't pleased because could not get A/C back "on the line" because we were short of replacement drive shafts. So I said I would sign if Engineering Officer would over sign me which he wouldn't when he saw the worn splines."

Situations like this were not uncommon; often the hierarchy demanded corners be cut if the aircraft were needed. It was down to the professionalism of the engineers to resist such dangerous practices, and in the process save lives. Luckily, the Jet Provost, being relatively simple and robust, had the ability to soak up a certain amount of 'bad practice' between major servicings. But aircraft losses were more often than not down to aircrew as Mal recalls:

"I did go on a "burial parade" in the cemetery up from Ulleskelf to the Barkston Ash – Tadcaster Rd. A student pilot had tried to under fly pylon electric cables somewhere near Scunthorpe to best of my knowledge, and crashed and killed himself just prior to the Entry he was on getting their Wings. Apparently it was a 'Dare Devil' thing they did till this unfortunately went wrong and he didn't give himself enough clearance. Was a sorry sight to see them polish up the Battam Carrier Coal wagon with his coffin draped with Union Jack and his 'Big Hat' and sword I think. I was on the firing party which sent off a volley as his coffin was lowered into the ground, and half the mourners nearly fell in with shock of [the] loud bang from the dozen or so of us 'Bods' firing the .303 le Enfield rifle."

RAF Church Fenton and No.7 FTS was reactivated in 1979 as a direct consequence of the introduction of the Tornado. Throughout the 1970s Flying Training had been slowly reduced, especially during the years of détente, as it looked like the Cold War would thaw. However, the introduction of the SS-20 coupled with events in central Asia, especially Afghanistan, forced NATO into a major defence re-think. A new Lightning squadron was announced along with weapons upgrades for Phantom and the arming of the Hawk with AIM-9L missiles, all intended as a stop-gap measure for Britain's air defence. New technology would be on line soon but as *The Under-Secretary of State for Defence for the Royal Air Force,* Mr Geoffrey Pattie, pointed out:

XN508 T3A. All RAF Church Fenton aircraft carried the 'CF' logo on the fin. (BigBird Aviation)

A fine shot of fleet 132 over the keys at RAF Church Fenton.

'The pilot shortage which we inherited on coming to power has not been allowed to prejudice the improvements planned to the RAF air defence forces. It is our firm intention to keep the air defence front line up to strength at all times. Steps to remedy the pilot shortage have already been taken by the opening of a third basic flying training school last year at Church Fenton to increase our training capacity. However, fully trained pilots are not produced overnight, and it will take time for these measures to take effect.'

House of Commons Deb, 23 June 1980, vol. 987 cc35-164.

Church Fenton received a new lease of life, and was to operate T.Mk.3A and T.Mk.5A Jet Provosts for a further ten years. Flt Lt John Letton, a student at Church Fenton in the mid-1980s, remembers some of the limitations surrounding the aircraft:

"The climb to FL250 to conduct 2 x 8 turn spins was for an air test only; I cannot remember the requirements for syllabus spin training. The Unit Test Pilot (UTP) would take 'studes' along for the ride where possible and I well remember using my flying gloves to scrape off the thin veneer of ice that built up on the inside of the canopy. Using heating/demist would have taken too much power from the engine and prolonged the climb unduly! The JP3A really was gutless! Low level navs at 210 + 240 kts were the limit and a real bad weather abort was not conducted lightly - the Pennines could easily out climb a 3A.

"On a hot day the JP3A could only operate with 'half-tips' fuel load as the temperature reduced the thrust on the engine. With the reduced power the aircraft could not safely clear the runway barrier and therefore couldn't carry a full fuel load.

"Once we were streamed fast-jet, after about 100 hrs flying, we progressed onto the JP5A to conduct the Group 1/Phase 1 portion of the course. After some ground school, we got the chance to fly the 'hot rod'. The difference in performance was quite remarkable with the added bonus of pressurisation making life quieter and more comfortable. The first climb had us students 'water skiing' behind the jet, trying desperately to keep up with the aircraft with its vastly superior climb rate. Best of all was how it pampered our egos; the canopy was electrically operated and once opened, the left elbow rested naturally on the cockpit sill to give the budding pilot a nonchalant air whilst taxiing back from a sortie. This was especially so if passing in front of the viewing enclosure on the south side of Fenton, passed after landing on runway 16! However, the JP5A was short on legs at low level. If I remember correctly, 40 minutes a low level was a normal maximum although being a pure turbojet, it was very economical at altitude.

"The Jet Provost could carry two 10lbs panniers for the crew to store essentials if they were on land-a-way. As you can appreciate 10lbs is nothing, especially by the time you have loaded a pair of shoes and your wash kit. Everything had to be crammed in before the pannier was pip-pinned onto the back of the engine door. By the time you had finished your sortie the engine had 'cooked' your gear; any creases you had inadvertently introduced into you kit was then there for life."

The first Royal Air Force ground school training course for the Shorts Tucano began on 16 October 1989, with flying training commencing on 4 December 1989. No.7 FTS was disbanded on 31 March 1992; however, the station operates a reduced flying service utilised by York University Air Squadron.

Not all aircraft were operated by *ab initio* training units, many stations carried a number of Jet Provosts for handling qualifications such as 'Spin-ex' and for tactical

XP547 T.Mk4 of the No.1 Tactical Weapons Unit at RAF Brawdy. The unit was one of the last to be operating the '4s'. (Pete James)

If only!

close support tutors. No.6 FTS in its navigation role has already been noted; however, others require mention. The College of Air Warfare stationed at RAF Manby was one such unit. It had inherited a number of aircraft from different units as they had closed down, operating a varying number of T.Mk.3s and T.Mk.4s until its eventual demise in 1974. Elements of the unit were later lodged at Leeming as the Refresher Flying School. The Central Air Traffic School at RAF Shawbury was formed on 11 February 1963 and originally operated a small fleet of Piston Provosts and Vampires. By 1974 these had been replaced by a fleet of T.Mk.4 aircraft. They were essentially used to give the trainee ATC staff something real to worry about, flying in continuous circuit or performing airfield movements. The school remains at Shawbury but the live element the T.Mk.4 provided was retired in June 1989. T.Mk.4s were also used in a supporting role with the Tactical Weapons Unit at RAF Brawdy until 1978 and then until 1990 with the re-badged No.1 Tactical Weapons Unit, again at Brawdy. One other enigmatic posting for the Jet Provost occurred in 1965 when three T.Mk.4s, straight from production, were dispatched to Tengah. The aircraft formed the Jet Provost Trials Unit, investigating the use of Forward Air Control (a full account by the Units CO can be found in Appendix One).

It is important at this point to remember T.Mk.5s were being taken on strength from the early 1970s, often displacing the T.Mk.4s. These aircraft were either relegated to the ground-based training role at Halton, Cosford, and similar, or scrapped. However, the T.Mk.5 also appeared as a number of variants, often dependant on the training role they were to perform. XS230, officially coded the T.Mk.5P, or Jet Provost Mk.4½ as it became known at Boscombe Down, remained with A&AEE after initial testing. It was absorbed into the fleet of ancient, non-standard types, which regularly caused the

XS230 T.Mk.4½! A&AEE 'inherited' this hybrid after the development programme for the T.Mk.5. This aircraft was routinely spun during the Empire Test Pilots course at Boscombe Down.

engineers no end of headaches. Whilst at Boscombe, the aircraft was routinely spun as part of the Empire Test Pilots course; indeed, this stomach-churning feat was filmed for a BBC documentary in 1985. However, it is the comments of the engineering team [a familiar story to the author] that are worth repeating here:

> 'Although the Jet Provost XS230 was to be used for the first dual demonstration, there had been some doubt that it would ever emerge from the distant hangar at Boscombe Down where it was undergoing an extensive overhaul; as one of the ETPS tutors put it: 'The only way that thing will ever fly is if it falls off its jack'. But emerge it did, a tribute to the men who have the difficult task of maintaining the varied ETPS fleet. John Winder, the civilian in charge, conceded that the Jet Provost is typical of the problems of keeping what is in effect an obsolescent aircraft airworthy: 'it's a hybrid, being a mixture of Mk.4 and Mk.5, so it has problems of interchangability and spares'.'

Test Pilot Brian Johnson, p.97.

Initially aircraft were manufactured to T.Mk.5 production standard; unfortunately, they were released to service just as the RAF were upgrading their communications systems. It became clear by mid-1972 that the aircraft, and incidentally the T.Mk.3 fleet, would require a substantial avionics update to remain effective.

> 'Mr. Green
> asked the Minister of State for Defence whether, in view of the shortage of aircraft repair work at the Preston factory of the British Aircraft Corporation, there are plans to allocate more defence repair work to that firm.

> 'Lord Balniel
> Following preliminary studies by BAC on a major avionics refit for the RAF's Jet Provost training aircraft, it has been decided that, subject to satisfactory contract arrangements, BAC should also carry out the work of incorporating the new equipment in the aircraft. This should help to ensure a viable workload for its Preston factory.'

House of Commons Debate, 26 October 1972, vol. 843 c356W.

Throughout 1973/5 the fleet was systematically modified. The work included a new instrument panel with additional indicators and cockpit lighting, the inclusion of a standby UHF radio and a series of navigational aids. Ninety-three aircraft were modified during the programme, along with seventy T.Mk.3s.

The T.Mk.5B was used in the Navigators course run by No.6 FTS, based at RAF Finningley, from late 1970. This aircraft conformed to Post-Modification 1791 and was the most noticeably different of the type. Firstly, the aircraft had wing tip-tanks giving the aircraft an extra ninety-six gallons of available fuel. This extra fuel enabled a further useful thirty minutes or so to be added to a standard navigation sortie. The aircraft also lacked the longitudinal strakes fitted to each side of the nose and the longitudinal fence under each intake, made unnecessary by the tip tanks. It also lacked the roughened outboard leading edges introduced to minimise the oscillation encountered during a spin.

It wasn't all training or training related operations. During the late 1950s - early 1960s a larger and larger proportion of front line aircraft were being displayed in formation at airshows. Events such as the twenty-two Hunter loop at Farnborough in 1958 caused a sensation, it also caused the RAF a severe headache. And when aircraft

A nice air-to-air shot of fleet 45, a Cranwell Jet Provost.

such as the Lightning joined the fray, the Ministry put its foot down. From then on the majority of display teams were to be from training units, a legacy that prevails today with the Red Arrows.

'APPROACHING FROM YOUR LEFT.'

Once the Jet Provost reached service, it was not long before the flying instructors were forming display teams; in fact the first team appeared as 'The Sparrows' in 1958 at RAF Little Rissington and comprised four T.Mk.1s. The team had flown four Piston Provosts the previous season; however, they took the opportunity to converted to the new jet-powered aircraft on their initial delivery. The Piston Provost livery was the standard training colours, silver with yellow bands on the rear fuselage and wings; however, the jet-powered Sparrows were white topped, with a striking red underside – clearly, all-through jet training was something to celebrate and recognise. The team performed at the 1958 Society of British Aviation Companies (SBAC) at Farnborough; naturally, Percival were happy to not miss a major sales opportunity, supplying ground support. At the end of the 1958 season the Sparrows disbanded; however, the T.Mk.1 did make display appearances the following year when a pair, named 'The Redskins', flew the UK circuit.

In 1960, as the new advanced T.Mk.3s were appearing at CFS and other FTS around the country, a new team, 'The Pelicans', was formed. It took its name from the CFS mascot the Pelican – the mythical bird of learning. The team were adopted as the RAF's official representative, operating four silver and red aircraft, until in 1962 they were replaced by a flight of T.Mk.4s. At the end of the season a further aircraft was added to the display team and it received a new name and colour scheme, all-over red – 'The Red Pelicans' were born. By 1964 the line-up had been increased to six aircraft and the Red Pelicans were presented as the RAF's 'premier aerobatic team'.

The original Red Pelican team of Central Flying School 1962

'The 1964 "Red Pelican Fledglings" foregathered early in February, when six pilots and ten ground personnel were selected from volunteers at the Central Flying School. Formation practice commenced with three aircraft with the pilots practicing basic manoeuvres in Echelon, Line-Abreast and Line-astern positions. As experience was gained, the number of aircraft was increased until, finally after much hard work, the complete formation of six aircraft was flown for the first time in late March.'

The Red Pelicans (TJ 205 JUNE 1964)

That year the team displayed at twenty-five shows around the UK, and at shows in Norway, Holland, Belgium and France. The aircraft, including innovative smoke generating equipment, performed well; however, at SBAC Farnborough in September 1964 the team unintentionally encountered their replacements. Throughout the week the Red Pelicans flew a co-ordinated display with the Yellowjacks, from RAF Valley. The Yellowjacks were stationed at No.4 FTS Valley, flying the Folland Gnat. The Gnat was a tiny aircraft but extremely manoeuvrable, some said so small you actually '*put it on rather than climbed in*', making it ideal for exciting displays. The following year the Gnat team was re-designated the Red Arrows, knocking the Red Pelicans from their official status; however, this did not deter many flying training schools from forming their own teams, and the Pelicans soldiered on, albeit in reduced numbers. The surviving aircraft were given a slightly darker shade of red and were relegated to 'non-smoke' displays.

From 1969 the RAF had been receiving the T.Mk.5, a number, naturally, making their way to Little Rissington. The Red Pelicans were duly equipped with the new airframes, and flew displays between 1970-1973 before they too were disbanded. Groundcrew comprised two engine mechanics, Allen Smallman & John Radge, an airframe specialist Dave Wickens and for the first time an armaments tech., Gordon Parkin. The 1970 flight team comprised Flt Lts Terry Francis, Bruce Donnelly, Peter Langham & Robert Lewis. The Pelicans were not the only Jet Provost team in this period: there was a veritable 'explosion' of teams representing operating units, occasionally in competition for airshow slots.

RAF Linton-on-Ouse was host to two display teams. Four T.Mk.4s were flown by No.1 FTS as the 'Gin-Four' from 1963, renaming as 'Linton Gin' for their last season in 1969. The name allegedly originated from the initials of three of the four founder members. The following year flew a four ship of T.Mk.5s known as 'The Blades', a reference to the swords in the station's crest; however, they were disbanded in 1973.

The College of Air Warfare at RAF Manby operated a number of Jet Provosts and naturally were eager to demonstrate their skills. Subsequently a team known as 'The Magistrates' represented the unit for two seasons between 1965-1967. The team name was a play on words: the initials of Jet Provost being JP, equating to 'Justice of the Peace', hence 'Magistrates'. However, this was not to be a permanent arrangement, as mid-way through 1968 the name was changed to the 'Macaws', an acronym of the establishment <u>Ma</u>nby <u>C</u>ollege of <u>A</u>ir <u>W</u>arfare. For their first outing the aircraft was painted grey with red tailfin, rudder and tip tanks. By the time of their final season in 1973 the aircraft were wearing standard training colours, with a black macaw stencilled on the nose, forward of the intakes. No. 2 FTS at RAF Syerston flew a four-ship team of T.Mk.3s and then T.Mk.4s known as the Vipers, named, not unsurprisingly, after the Viper engine. The team represented the unit in 1968 and 1969 until they were rather indignantly replaced by a team armed with a pair of Chipmunks!

Between 1970 and 1973 No.3 Flying Training School, by now based at RAF Leeming, , operated a pair of Jet Provosts, initially T.Mk.4s then T.Mk.5s, named

The 1964 Red Pelican Team in six T.Mk.4s.

The Red Pelicans were equipped with T.Mk.5s for display between 1970-1973.

Linton Gin. One of four T.Mk.4s that were flown from RAF Linton-on-Ouse until 1969. (John Ryan)

XR704 T.Mk.4 of the Macaws. Display team representing RAF Manby College of Air Warfare. (Bigbird Aviation)

One of the Gemini Pair taxiing in after practice at RAF Leeming

Gemini. The display featured formation and synchronised individual aerobatics and a number of 'opposition' manoeuvres – roulette was formally banned and removed from the sequence following a fatal Red Arrows accident. The highlight of the Gemini display incorporated into the full, rolling and flat show sequences was the signature Mirror formation. The composition of the team changed each year with Flight Lieutenants Ron Pattinson & Gordon Revell in 1971, Flight Lieutenants John Galyer and Dave Trusler in 1972, and Flight lieutenant Bob Thompson and Flying Officer Dusty Miller in 1973. The same principle applied to the ground crew who flew to and from shows with the team: Senior Aircraftsmen Colin Wadsworth and Bob Goodier supported the team in 1972, and Bob Goodier with Ron Anderson did so in 1973. The Swords comprised four T.Mk.5s and were recognisable by the thin blue fuselage flash, retained from the days of Gemini, and a gold sword running up the tail fin; as with Linton-on-Ouse, the sword was taken from the station crest. Squadron Leader Olly Knight managed Gemini and The Swords throughout the period 1973-74.

'SUCCESS TO EVERY GENTLEMAN THAT LIVES IN LINCOLNSHIRE'

Royal Air Force College Cranwell flew a team of T.Mk.3s, called the 'Cranwell Poachers', named after the folk song 'Lincolnshire Poacher' - the unofficial county anthem, in 1965 as a successor to their highly popular de Havilland Vampire display. However it was not until 1968 that the team represented the unit again and a full programme was flown from 1969, by then in T.Mk.4s, until 1970. For the 1971 season the team were renamed 'The Poachers' and equipped with T.Mk.5s. In 1973, the MOD decided to limit the number of Jet Provost teams the RAF were operating to one per year; the Poachers were disbanded.

Surprisingly, it was neither the hours nor disruption to training that brought about the demise of so many teams in the early 1970s. It was the direct result of

Gemini programme 1973

The centrepiece of the Gemini display a mirrored role.

Gemini was replaced for just one season in 1974 by 'The Swords', a four ship of T.Mk.5As. RAF Leeming.

The original Cranwell Poachers in T.Mk.3s (John Ryan)

an Organization of Arab Petroleum Exporting Countries (OAPEC) announcement informing the world that member countries along with Egypt and Syria were longer prepared to trade oil with countries sympathetic to Israel and the Yon Kippur War. When Arab nations took the opportunity to raise world oil prices, the effects were devastating to many economies, including the United Kingdom. At home, fuel rationing was imposed and the situation had repercussions for the MOD. All unnecessary flying was curtailed, including the aerobatic teams. To give some indication as to why this was the case, fuel totals for training below OCU level had been 23,397 million gallons in 1972/3, a phenomenal amount of avtur. However, up until then it had also been relatively cheap. So much so that many 'extra-curricular' activities were easily written off as 'CT' or crew training. Now, with the price doubling almost overnight, the defence budget could not stand the increase. For some the cuts did not go far enough, as the following debate demonstrates:

'10. Mr. Watkinson
asked the Secretary of State for Defence what plans he has to cut back the activities of display teams in the RAF.

'Mr. John
I have no plans at present further to curtail the activities of the RAF display teams beyond the significant reductions imposed last year by the need to conserve manpower, money and fuel.

'Mr. Watkinson
Will my hon. Friend say how many such display teams there are and what is their total cost? Will he confirm that the cost of running the Red Arrows last year was more than £800,000? One appreciates the technical skill of the Red Arrows, but is it advisable at the present time to continue their flying at that cost? Do these display teams have any significant effect upon recruitment?

'Mr. John

Six flying teams are at present organising and there is one ground display team. As for recruiting and value for money, without going into the precise costs at this stage I can assure my hon. Friend that we are satisfied that such displays of great expertise have a significant effect on recruiting and are worth while. However, we are always looking at ways of securing greater value for money.

'Mr. Costain

Does the Minister appreciate that his announcement is very welcome particularly in areas which have had the benefit of seeing these displays including events on the coast? Does he agree that it does a good deal for the RAF's prestige and a good deal to encourage youth to join the Royal Air Force?

'Mr. John

We believe that the exercise is worth while in terms of public relations for the Royal Air Force and in terms of recruitment.'

House of Commons Debate, 13 May 1975, vol. 892 c231.

One of those teams '*at present organising*' was the Poachers. They had received the go-ahead signal to re-form on 11 March 1975. Team selection had been ongoing through a series of 'fly-offs' since January. The final team for 1975 was Squadron Leader P. Curtin (No.1), Eddie Danks (No.2), Martin Stoner (No.3) and David Webley (No.4). During the 1975 season the Poachers flew thirty-four displays, of which five were overseas; one in France, two in Germany and two in the Channel Islands. Whilst the aircraft was often praised for its flying qualities in the hands of students, the same could not be said during displays:

'The Jet Provost is not the best formation aerobatic aircraft. For a start, it has a very straight wing and, of course, shows up any small line error in plan view. It is slow to accelerate, so power has to be anticipated very accurately. Join up manoeuvres have to be carefully planned, otherwise long delays occur and people think the show has finished!'

Or indeed during any manoeuvring:

'There is no power assistance to the flying controls and the stick loads are quite heavy. In fact, as an arm muscle-building course, a season with a Jet Provost team is excellent value. We are now all aces at arm wrestling.'

'The Poachers 1975', *Training Command Flight Safety Magazine*, Jan-Mar 1976

Undeterred by the physical nature of the display, the team were back in 1976, with an improved colour scheme and a thirty date show including Waddington, Upper Heyford, Whitby and Scarborough. All display flying was regulated by the team's Standard Operating Procedures, a set of rules and regulations governing providing guidance for every eventuality:

'29. Emergency Break.

'If another aircraft is approaching the formation and the leader is unable to take avoiding action with the complete formation he is to call an Emergency Break. The call is to be "Poachers Emergency Break – Go" and the team is to respond as follows:

The Poachers reformed in 1975, this time armed with the 'sportier' looking T.Mk.5A

Red Pelicans over Blackpool

'The Leader is to pull up vertically.
Numbers 2 and 3 are to pull upwards and away from the Leader.
Numbers 4, 5 and 6 are to push downwards and outwards from the Leader if height allows.

' 30. Mid-Air Collision.

'In the event of a mid-air collision, the damaged aircraft are to leave the formation each escorted, if possible, by a serviceable aircraft. Pilots of damaged aircraft are to carry out a low speed handling check at a safe height before attempting a landing.'

The team comprised five aircraft, each populated by one pilot and a groundcrew member. George Dobie was a Flight Line Mechanic at Cranwell from 1974-79 and recalls his time with the team:

"I don't have any photo's lying around as it was a long time ago and as we used to fly with the aircraft to each show cameras kind of got in the way of the "beer chits" for the post airshow functions! During my time on the team (1975-76), I spent virtually every weekend during the summer at airshows servicing my aircraft. The "Flying Circus" (or more aptly referred to as "alcoholics on tour") consisted of 5 aircraft (JP5A), 4 for the display and 1 spare. Obviously, there were 5 pilots and 5 groundcrew. The spare pilot gave the commentary. During my time we gave shows throughout the UK, France, Germany and the Channel Islands. I flew with Flt Lt Martin (Stumpy) Stoner and Flt Lt Dave Webley, both ex Lightning pilots who served together at RAF Gutersloh in Germany. When flying in transit to airshows the journey was never boring as they were both keen to keep up their "dog fighting" skills, thankfully I had a strong stomach! On leaving Cranwell Martin Stoner joined the "Red Arrows" I believe he ended his time as a Wg Cmdr flying Tornados. The team disbanded after the 76 season due to defence cuts."

One further display orientated item is required here – The Wright Jubilee Trophy. The trophy was presented in 1953 by the Royal Air Forces Association to the Air Council, to commemorate the fiftieth anniversary of the Wright Brothers' flight. Originally, the trophy competition took place at the Central Flying School, RAF Little Rissington, during July, in the form of an aerobatic contest between selected flying instructors from the Jet Flying Training Schools and the RAFC College, RAF Cranwell. Aircraft taking part in the early years included Meteors and Vampires with the competition becoming more Jet Provost-orientated by the early 1960s. Each pilot was required to execute a loop, slow roll, roll off the top of a loop, eight-point hesitation roll and vertical roll. In addition, each competitor was allowed two minutes in which to carry out a manoeuvre of his own choice. Originally, the winner was announced on the day but did not receive the trophy until 17 December, the anniversary of the Wrights' first flight.

And so, the Jet Provost can rightly claim to have been the cornerstone of flying training in the Royal Air Force, serving, as it did, for almost three decades. The aircraft did, however, see service outside the United Kingdom, becoming one of the few aviation success stories of post-war British industry. The development of that aircraft and its subsequent service in a number of conflict zones are the subject of the next chapter.

6.

Strikemaster!

In 1971, during a debate on the state of the aerospace industry, MP John Wilkinson stated:

> 'The Jet Provost Mk 5s have been introduced into Royal Air Force service without being fitted with rocket rails or gyro gunsights or guns for weapon training or for operations. This is a mistake philosophically, because weaponry should be introduced as early as possible into the pilot's flying training but industrially it is a mistake because, if this facility were provided, even retrospectively, it would provide valuable new work—and that is what is needed now. If there is any shortfall on Jet Provosts in the years ahead, I hope that they will be made up with the weapon-equipped and slightly more potent 167 Strikemaster variant.

> 'I have also made other proposals about a jet element for the reserves, and if Strikemaster were ordered that would be valuable. There is a danger that the Strikemaster line, which has been very profitable—over 100 units have been sold to a number of air forces—will come to an end. If we only had a further Government order for the Royal Air Force, further developments of this most excellent training and cheap close support aircraft could be provided which would provide more work and more export potential.'

House of Commons Debate, 15 December 1971, vol. 828 cc573-650.

That requirement for the RAF Reserve, or for that matter, regular service was never realised; however, the Strikemaster variant remained in production until May 1988. By then 156 had been constructed. The aircraft formed the backbone of many small air forces' Counter Insurgency (COIN), ground support and jet training capabilities, some participating in action. The story of the Strikemaster is the final chapter in the military history of the aircraft. However, we must travel back to 1960 and an account of the first Jet Provost export derivatives, the T.51 and T.52, to make sense of why so many later orders were placed from the Middle East.

You will recall that, during the development of the T.Mk.3, Hunting Percival pilots embarked on a number of sales and demonstration tours around the world; and whilst no immediate sales were generated, the concept of an armed version of the aircraft was effectively proven. By mid-1960, the first of a number of orders for foreign forces was nearing completion at Luton. The Royal Ceylonese Air Force ordered twelve aircraft, designated the T.51, to perform both trainer and light ground attack roles.

The Royal Ceylonese Air Force ordered 12 T.51 armed Jet Provosts, the first country to do so. (Hunting Aircraft Ltd)

The T.51 had two .303 machine guns, one mounted on either side, with 600 rounds each. Two stores racks and four fixed pylons could carry a further combination of rockets and 25lb bombs under the wings. A gun camera was fitted in the nose and two reflector gunsights were located in front of each pilot. Just a few weeks later on 1 February 1960, during a routine formation practice, disaster struck for Squadron Leader (then Pilot Officer) Noel Howard Lokuge of the RCyAF. The event was later recorded by Michael C. Bennett.:

"One fine day, I was No.3, in a formation of 6 JPs practicing for the independence day fly past, which was on the 4th of February. Soon after take off and at about 1000ft up I noticed that my aircraft was falling out of the formation. I realised my engine had flamed out, I tried two relights but unfortunately the engine did not respond. By that time I had to turn the aircraft away from the Negombo Town, a highly populated town, and glided the aircraft to a safe area over the Negombo lagoon. I lost a lot of height at the same time. When I was clear and at 350 ft I used the face blind handle and ejected."

The accident was witnessed from the ground by John Cooper:

"We were working on Staging Aircraft Servicing Flight at RAF Katunayake (formerly RAF Negombo) in Ceylon. Our role was to see in and out all the visiting Military aircraft and to give assistance to the Civvy Airlines if required (usually via Brown Envelopes!). I recall several of us standing on the pan looking at this display between SASF and the RCyAF hangars, the 6 ships were formating SE of Negombo Town on a SE heading, I recall the six JPs banking and one didn't, it fell like a brick, the pilot 'banged out' at fairly low level, we heard that he was OK. The odd thing is that this story is recorded in my diary which sits in a suitcase in a Hastings hold 8,000' down in the Indian Ocean 1.5 NM E of the Island of Gan."

The Sudan ordered 4 T.51s plus ground equipment and spares cover in July 1961. (Hunting Aircraft Ltd)

Thankfully, not all flights ended in disaster; and by July 1961 the Sudan Air Force signed a contract for four aircraft complete with ground equipment and a certain amount of spares coverage, whilst Kuwait ordered six aircraft in August the same year. Pilots from The Sudan were trained at No.2 FTS at Syerston throughout the winter months on the T.Mk.3, which must have been quite an experience for the young men. Once the order was completed, the four aircraft were delivered by ferry flight, in itself an epic journey as the following company press release demonstrates:

'The aircraft will be flown to Khartoum on Thursday 17th October [1961]. The aircraft will be delivered to the Sudan by pilots of Nos. 1 and 2 Flying Training Stations under the leadership of Flight Lieutenant David McCann, deputy leader of the Central Flying School Jet Provost Aerobatic Team stationed at Little Rissington.

'This flight will cover a total of about 3,500 miles from Thorney Island to Khartoum via: Dijon – Orange – Sardinia – Malta – Benina – El Adem – Alexandria – Cairo – Luxor and Wadi Halfa. The other pilots will be:-

'Flt.Lt. Hugh W.J. Rigg. No.1 F.T.S., Linton-on-Ouse.
Flg.Off. Roger M. Austin. No.1 F.T.S., Linton-on-Ouse.

'Flt.Lt. Christopher Thorman. No.2 F.T.S., Syerston.
Flt.Lt. Ian Hamilton. No.2 F.T.S., Syerston.
M/Plt. Hedley Shepherd. No.2 F.T.S., Syerston.'

By mid-1960 it had become clear that the benefits of the more powerful T.Mk.4 currently under development for the Ministry had potential beyond the UK market. Offering the Jet Provost with a new, powerful powerplant proved attractive to a

The T.51 was capable of carrying four small bombs and two rockets under each wing. It was also armed with intake mounted .303 machine guns. (Hunting Aircraft Ltd)

Kuwait Air Force T.51. Contract signed August 1961. (Hunting Aircraft Ltd)

small number of foreign air forces. First to accept the new T.52 was The Sudan, complimenting their T.51 fleet with an order, signed by Abdel Bagi Mohammed on 2 May 1962, for a further four aircraft. By October 1962 BAC was taking out two page adverts in *Flight International* boasting '*Venezuela Chooses The Jet Provost: Yet another country orders the Jet Provost all-through jet trainer*'. Further sales were achieved through negotiation with Iraq's new President, Abdul Salam Arif, a major reformer of the country throughout his three years in control. A contract was signed with BAC in March 1964 and by the autumn Iraq was poised to receive the first of twenty T.52s. The first aircraft were delivered by ferry flight from Luton in August 1964; fulfilling the contract took just over eighteen months. A further eight aircraft were operated in South Yemen, their story is more complicated and the background to that is worth presenting here.

Prior to withdrawal from Aden and the newly formed Federation of South Arabia, the British detachment undertook the training of local military forces. By early 1967 this included a small contingency air wing – South Arabia Air Force (SAAF). Financed by the British Government and supported by Airwork and service personnel, the undertaking was extensive, as Secretary of State for Foreign Affairs Mr George Brown revealed:

'Concerning the Army, we have informed the Federal Government that we are prepared to pay for the South Arabian Army to be re-equipped with more modern small arms—for example, the self-loading rifle instead of the Lee Enfield—to obtain additional armoured

Venezuelan Air Force T.52. The T.52 took advantage of the development of the T.Mk.4 for the RAF by using a similar engine. (Hunting Aircraft Ltd)

cars and field artillery, and to have the assistance of a British military aid mission after independence which will help with advice and training. We will also help with such things as communications, base maintenance, and with some medical staff for the Federal forces hospital. All of this represents a very important strengthening of the Armed Forces of South Arabia.

'As regards the Air Force, we have agreed to finance the provision and operation of eight Hunter aircraft, which would be additional to the jet Provost ground attack aircraft which the Air Force is already to have. The continued incitement to subversion in the States outside Aden, and the threat from across the frontier, in cynical disregard of the interests of the people and of Britain's departure from the territory, create a clear need to ensure that a South Arabian Air Force is equipped more powerfully than it would otherwise need to be. We have accepted this need and decided to help to meet it.'

House of Common Debate, 19 June 1967, vol. 748 cc1125-262.

The aircraft 'ear-marked' for the SAAF were taken from the current production batch of T.Mk.4s destined for the RAF. All were modified up to T.52 standard whilst on the line. As the last British troops were being airlifted from Aden, the South Arabian Federation proclaimed itself the Peoples Democratic Republic of South Yemen; at the time only half the T.52 order was in place but by late December all were operational. Tensions grew with limited internal operations against local militia, but throughout 1968 the Saudi Arabian ruling body lodged numerous complaints against T.52 incursions into their airspace. Luckily the chance of hostilities was negated by the fact that the vast majority of pilots on both sides were either RAF detachment or British Government sponsored.

Unfortunately the South Yemeni Government wanted counter-insurgency operations to be undertaken in North Yemen in an attempt to slow the frequent border infringements. The British Government made strong protests, lacking a policy covering the use of British nationals employed by the South Yemeni government outside its political borders. As a direct consequence, the South Yemen government cancelled all contracts with foreign pilots, uniform or civilian, leaving the Air Force just one trained jet pilot. The history of what happened to the aircraft is difficult to ascertain; however, one aircraft was written off in a landing accident in 1968. A further aircraft succumbed to ground fire and at least one aircraft ingested debris from a rocket attack after exceeding the minimum safety height for that weapon. Interestingly, one aircraft did survive. Built in 1964 as part of the RAF order, XS228 as it was originally serial numbered, transferred to 27 MU Aircraft Supply & Servicing Depot, RAF Shawbury. In 1967 the aircraft returned to Warton, where it was modified to T.52 standard and delivered to The Yemen. From 1975 it was in the service of the Singapore Air Force until returning to British in 1983 in private hands. G-PROV, as it is now registered, is currently the only T.52 airworthy anywhere in the world.

Sales of both aircraft were a little disappointing, twenty T.51 and fifty-one T.52 in all; and, as has been mentioned, a number of those came from RAF reserves under British Government finance. However, the potential of the Jet Provost variant had been demonstrated. Aircraft in South Yemen had seen action on a number of occasions and given a good account, even G-PROV received battle damage. Now with even more

Iraq Air Force T.52. The Iraqi government ordered 20 aircraft in March 1964, the contract took 18 months to complete. (British Aircraft Corporation)

potential markets opening for light ground attack aircraft, BAC set about developing the ultimate JP variant – the Strikemaster.

DEVELOPMENT HISTORY

The Strikemaster, powered by the Viper 535 turbojet, was a far superior aircraft to the BAC-145. Visibly, little had changed, save the addition of underwing stores points; however, the aircraft structure was substantially strengthened. The range was dramatically increased with the addition of tip tanks carrying forty-eight Imperial gallons each (a similar fit to the T.Mk.5 flown by 6 FTS). This could be further complimented by fitting external tanks to the four underwing hard points, carrying seventy-five Imperial gallons (Outbd) and fifty Imperial Gallons (Inbd).

The underwing stores' capacity was formidable: 3,000lb could be carried, to support a variety of operational requirements. The eight underwing points were capable of four 750lb and four 200lb payloads, which could include four 18 Tube

The Strikemaster could carry a wide range of weaponry as this RNZAF Mk.88 demonstrates. (RNZAF Official, via Air Force Museum, Christchurch, NZ)

SNEB 68mm rockets, four 500lb bombs, two .5in mini-gun pods combined with two SNEB Tubes, fifty gallon napalm tanks or twenty-four SURA R 80 rockets and eight 20lb fragmentation bombs. Naturally, the wing structure was considerably beefier than the T.Mk.5, to cope with the loads. The weapons compliment was completed with two 7.62mm machine guns mounted longitudinally in the lower fairing of the intake and two spent case ejector chutes were provisioned on either underside. From the early 1970s a two-gunned machine gun pod, developed by Portsmouth Aviation and intended to be carried on a multitude of aircraft, was also cleared for operation. The Strikemaster could carry four at a time.

The ASV-20 Viper 535 powerplant greatly increased the performance of the Strikemaster over its T.Mk.5 predecessor. The frontal compressor area was increased, necessitating a new and larger intake duct; the jet pipe diameter was also increased by 1.5in to 16.5in. All this gave additional thrust, whilst negating the loss in power experienced with the introduction of the pressurised front end. The end result was a maximum speed (clean) of 418kt, maximum range 1,250 miles, with an initial climb rate of 52,50ft per minute topping out at a 40,000ft service ceiling. The origins of the name are difficult to ascertain; however, it seems likely that the BAC sales team first coined the name in the late 1960s.

All orders contained a high degree of customer requirements, leading to the plethora of marks now recognised. Key differences were, in the main, avionics packages including fixed reflector or gyro-compensated gun sights, VHF, UHF, ADF, DME, ILS and TACAN, spawning twelve different marks. Naturally, each type of weapons load had to be checked for compatibility with the avionics fit, initiating a series of tests undertaken at Warton to ensure arrangements were safe. The problem is that transmitting by aircraft radio can potentially detonate or release aircraft stores, as can a static discharge from personnel working on the aircraft. The trials report written after investigative work undertaken in late September 1970 on G-27-191, destined for Kenya, describes the situation:

'b. Loading and Unloading Procedure

'Past experience shows that the most favourable conditions for pick-up normally occur during the loading and unloading phase; therefore, it is the most hazardous. Personnel handling the weapon and making firing line connections act as aerials and assist the transfer of energy to the EEDs. Several factors affect the amount of pick-up; weather conditions, the electrical properties of the human body, whether certain parts of the aircraft or weapon are touched or not, and all these vary from one occasion to another. All possible steps, therefore, should be taken to reduce the external RF environment during loading and unloading phases.'

Electromagnetic Compatibility of Weapons Fitted to BAC-167 Strikemaster MK 87 Aircraft. MAS Ref: AV/583/029, 20 January 1970.

Further work was undertaken in 1970 on the seat arrangements for the Jet Provost range, including Strikemaster. This required the existing Mk.4P seat to be upgraded to Mk.6PB, and in so doing make major improvements in the low level and medium speed areas, clearly intended for the improved performance of the T.Mk.5 and Strikemaster. Initial modifications included the incorporation of a rocket motor with approximately 4000lb thrust from a .25 second burn time. The initial tests, both static and from Martin-Bakers Meteor aircraft, were successful. However, the seat improvements were not incorporated into the aircraft. This did not, however, deter sales abroad.

THE MIDDLE EAST

With TSR2 and other contracts gone or unlikely to develop past the experimental stage, the pressure on the BAC sales team to discover new product outlets was huge. Civil aircraft sales were beginning to take shape, especially the BAC 1-11 and to a lesser extent VC10; but the military division was in a very poor state. Incredibly, BAC managed to turn a bit part (supplying a small number of refurbished Canberras) offered by the Americans in Saudi Arabia into the company's biggest contract.

The order was, at the time, one of the largest post-war contracts ever won by a British defence contractor and it continues to be the mainstay of BAe after Airbus commitments. What made the contract extraordinary was that it was won from under the nose of the United States. True, Raytheon was to supply a missile system as part of the deal, but it was nowhere near what Washington had hoped for. Prior to 1965 the Royal Saudi Air Force was a minor league player on the Middle East stage. The force had been reorganised in 1950 and just two years later began to receive 'assistance' from the United States. Along with military advisors, the US supplied a squadron of refurbished F.84 Sabres in the Fighter/Ground Attack role, an arrangement that was to last nearly fifteen years. Naturally, when it was first mooted that the Saudi Government wanted to increase its home defence effectiveness, most analysts considered the US defence community would benefit from any ensuing work, especially since the British Government had been implicated in fighting along Saudi Arabia's border with North Yemen. Luckily for BAC, by then the US contingency operating from Dhahran had

Mk.80. Saudi Arabia was the first of many to order the Strikemaster.

given a poor account of themselves, especially in the ground attack role. Subsequent discussions with the Kingdom throughout 1962/3 ensured that some enquires for aircraft were made with the UK. By 1963 the Saudi Defence Ministry was convinced it required Lightning interceptors rather than Northrop F-5s or the late running offer of Mirage III. The association between British expertise and the defence of the Saudi Kingdom was announced to Parliament on 21 December 1965:

'The Parliamentary Secretary to the Ministry of Aviation (Mr. John Stonehouse)

'With your permission, Mr. Speaker, and that of the House, I would like to make a statement. I have to tell the House that the Government of Saudi Arabia have this morning announced that a consortium of British firms has secured the major part of the order for their new complete air defence system. The remainder of the system will be provided by American firms and we have had valuable cooperation from the United States Administration in formulating the joint programme. The value of the British components in the order, including Lightning and Jet Provost aircraft, radar and data handling equipment, is over £100 million, from which over £75 million will accrue to this country as export earnings.

'This is a great achievement for the three British firms concerned, namely, the British Aircraft Corporation Ltd., Associated Electrical Industries, and Airwork Services Ltd. and it demonstrates that our aircraft and electronics industries have really first-class equipment to offer.'

504 Strikemaster Mk.81 South Yemen Air Force at Hurn 22-Jul-69. (Peter Vine)

House of Commons Debate, 21 December 1965, vol. 722 cc1873-6.

Within that initial order was a requirement for twenty-five BAC-167 Strikemasters, to perform light attack and training duties. The final two airframes was delivered by ferry flight during the last week of September 1968. The order did not go unnoticed by other countries in the region, and soon the Strikemaster order book was filling up. With stiff competition from the Macchi 326, the type out-performed the BAC-167 in every area save basic training; BAC knew that production turn around and costs would be pivotal. In 1969 the price of a Strikemaster was £180,000, not including weapons package. This was the triple-role layout for basic training ground attack/COIN and reconnaissance utilising a Vinten Camera pod. All this could, whilst production included work on the T.Mk.5 for the RAF, be achieved in fourteen months. On 1 June 1967 it was announced that the Air Force of Sudan and Sultanate of Muscat and Oman had both placed orders for the aircraft.

THE SUDAN

Interestingly, the Sudanese Air Force was supplied with Mk.55 aircraft, technically a T.Mk.5, following the earlier numbering convention adopted for overseas aircraft. The aircraft were fitted with intake machine guns and spent case chutes, as was standard on the Strikemaster; however, everything else essentially followed the BAC-145. It is likely that the original price tag of £150,000, including all ground support equipment, drove the decision; however, the five constructed were the only ones of their type delivered. The Sudanese aircraft were ferry-flighted to the region in mid-1969, but by then BAC had 'branded' the aircraft – successfully distancing the Strikemaster from the RAF trainer.

MUSCAT AND OMAN

Answering a request by the Sultan of Oman in 1957 for help, the British Government set up and equipped the Sultan of Oman's Armed Forces. Interestingly, the first aircraft on inventory were four Piston Provosts. A series of minor rebellions, uprisings and insurrections, including the Buraimi Oasis incident of 1952 to 1955, Jebel and Akhdar war between 1957 and 1959, both supported by Saudi Arabia, left the area politically weak. The Omani forces were complemented, on occasion, by SAS troops brought in from Indonesia, prompting the Saudis to protest at British involvement – a protest, incidentally, that nearly scuppered the 1965 Saudi Arabian deal. By 1962 the Dhofar region of the country was in open revolt against the Sultan. That year the Dhofar Liberation Front (DLF), supported again by Saudi arms and equipment, attacked the airbase at Salalah and destroyed many vehicles connected with the burgeoning oil industry. Supported by the North Yemen Government, itself a Republic essentially propped up by Nasser in Egypt, the struggles were part of a general surge of Arab nationalism. By 1964/5 the DLF had been schooled in hit and run techniques in Iraq and were causing some series problems in the west of Oman. The Aden Crisis' culmination in November 1967 with the mass evacuation of service dependants and personnel, primarily by air, did little to help the situation. Neither did the subsequent creation of South Yemen on 26 November 1967, bringing more unrest to the borders of Oman.

Earlier that year, Oman had decided to modernise and re-equip the air force and Strikemasters were ordered. *Flight International* that June perceptively commented

– *'The Sultanate, which occupies the south-eastern corner of the Saudi Arabian peninsula and abuts the South Arabian Federation, appears to be preparing itself for trouble'*. An initial undertaking was announced at the end of May 1967 and a further order placed on 2 May 1968, the twelve Mk.82 Strikemasters were subsequently delivered through 1969. Interestingly, that same year Yemen purchased four Mk.81 aircraft, complementing the existing force of T.51 & T.52.

The aircraft purchased by the Oman all saw active service, a few accounts giving a flavour of the operations concerned have been supplied by Richard Ansley, who was station there at the time:

"The aircraft were based at Salalah during the Dhofar War and flown north to Seeb for depot level servicing consisting of "equalised servicing" 1,2.3 & 4. They flew via RAF Masirah and usually carried 16 SURA rockets and 2 X 75 gallon underwing tanks as well as 500 rounds for each gun. This was in case the Adoo (enemy) were encountered en route. The same was carried on the return journey. Sometimes they would carry bombs for training at the ranges in the north. On occasion they would take ground fire in and out of Salalah. The attached photo [see below] is 419 which was hit by a SAM-7 while on ops with the army. The pilot refused to eject as there was no helicopter in the area to rescue him from the Adoo and the aircraft was still flying. He continued to fly it for about 20 minutes to an Iranian base code named 'Manston' and landed it there. Just shows that they were built like the proverbial brick s**t house!!

"There is a story that I believe is true, told to me by a Skyvan pilot. That a Strikie returning from Seeb arrived overhead Salalah at the onset of an attack. The Adoo used to fire mortars into Salalah in threes and then disappear into a cave before anybody could pinpoint their position. The pilot saw the first round hit and was lucky enough to spot the second round being fired. He then fired all 16 SURA at the point where he thought the

401 Strikemaster Mk.82 Sultan of Oman Air Force, Hurn 15-Jan-69 (Peter Vine)

Oman 419 at Manston (code name for an Iranian base in Oman) after a SAM-7 hit. The aircraft continued to fly for another 20 minutes. (Richard Ansley)

cave was that the Adoo were firing from. The third round was never fired and apparently the army confirmed that he had successfully buried them in what was left of the cave. A case of being in the right place at the right time and looking in the right direction!"

Of all the world sales of Strikemaster variants, those in the service of the SOAF saw more action and flew more operational hours than many other aircraft put together. When the type was finally retired in 1997, some of the surviving airframes had less than ten hours fatigue life left in them! Of the twenty-five aircraft owned by Oman, five were sold on to the Singapore Air Defence Command in 1977; five crashed, one of those during an air test; four went on to be instructional airframe; seven were gate guardians for various airfields or on display in museums, whilst only three were actually lost to enemy action. One further example, Ser. No. 425, is now prevalent on the British airshow circuit as, appropriately, G-SOAF.

SINGAPORE AIR DEFENCE COMMAND

In January 1968 the Wilson Government announced further cuts in defence spending. Along with the usual cancellation of major projects, the UK's presence abroad was to be further reduced. All stations throughout the Far East, with the notable exception of Hong Kong, were to be abandoned by 1971, leaving just Mediterranean and European commitments. The withdrawal included Singapore and Malaysia and was to have far-reaching consequences. Over 70,000 servicemen were demobbed and once the withdrawal was complete a number of aircraft carriers were scrapped.

The announcement forced the Government of the Republic of Singapore to consider building its own air defence. In the second week of July 1968, a contract was signed with BAC in Singapore for sixteen BAC-167 Mk.84s, worth £3 million. By mid-1968 flight training had started at Seletar, using existing piston aircraft, in anticipation of the first Strikemasters. On 6 October 1969 the first wave of aircraft destined for Singapore's Air Defence Command left Warton, on an eleven day trip to Tengah; jet training started at the base in January 1970. By mid-1971 the new Air Arm – the Singapore Air Defence Command – was operational. The Mk.84s performed a dual role. They formed part of the flight training syllabus, ensuring pilots were ready for Hunter conversion and provided close support training for both land and sea forces.

BAC also received an order from the Kuwait Air Force during this period. Originally operating the T.51, the air force had been exploring a number of aircraft as a replacement since 1967, but plumped on twelve Mk.83 Strikemasters in 1969. The first was delivered by ferry flight via Akrotiri on 19 March 1970, the contract was fulfilled by mid-1971. By 1985 BAe, as the design authority had now become, accepted the remaining nine aircraft back to the UK and after two years refurbishment and storage the aircraft were resold to Botswana.

Following the tradition of 'colonial sales', the first two Mk.87 Strikemasters ordered by the Kenya Air Force (KAF) arrived at Eastleigh Airport, Nairobi, on 19 January 1971. Unusually, these aircraft and the four that followed formed the only

305 BAC 167 Strikemaster Singapore Air Defence Command. (British Aircraft Corporation)

Kuwait Air Force Mk.83. (British Aircraft Corporation)

front line combat squadron in the KAF at that time. Pilots started training for the Strikemaster with a basic course on the Scottish Aviation Bulldog, located in Britain. BAe accepted four of the six aircraft back in 1985, refurbished and then sold them on to the Botswana Defence Force Air Wing three years later.

'BLUNTY'

The Royal New Zealand Air Force (RNZAF) flew sixteen Mk.88 Strikemasters in the advanced jet and later ground attack training role, with the initial order for ten placed on 19 November 1970. The decision had not been easy. The RNZAF preferred the Strikemaster due to its proven ground attack and substantial forward, un-prepared strip operational capability, coupled with a more robust construction and side-by-side cockpit arrangement. The New Zealand Government hoped it would choose the Aermacchi MB326 currently being built under licence by the Commonwealth Aircraft Corporation for the Royal Australian Air Force; luckily for BAC, the Strikemaster won. The first batch of ten aircraft were shipped to New Zealand throughout early 1972, and on 26 May that year the aircraft were officially handed over to No.14 Squadron. Throughout April and May of 1972 the ground training school at Warton played host to a twenty-five strong detachment of No.14 Squadron personnel for a familiarisation and ground servicing course. Interestingly, the first aircraft were all fitted with the outdated canopy jettison system, rather than MDC, as trials were still

A rather over attended Mk.88 of the Royal New Zealand Air Force. (RNZAF Official, via Air Force Museum, Christchurch, NZ)

underway at this point at Boscombe Down; it had to be retro-fitted. A further six Strikemasters were introduced into service in 1976, when the Government decided to incorporate jet aircraft in the flying training syllabus. The aircraft became known as 'Blunty', the origin of which, as is so often the case with aviation folk law, is difficult to ascertain. However, a few theories have been put forward. Talking to crews in New Zealand, most considered the name originated from the amount of drag the front end caused, especially since there were a lot of dome-head rivets used in its construction. Strangely, Royal Air Force aircrew today class anyone who doesn't fly as 'Blunties'! You decide.

The Mk.88 was utilised heavily in the trainer and strike conversion role, replacing Vampire aircraft that had operated with No.75 Squadron since the late 1951. This included the use of the intake-mounted machine guns, the operation and servicing of which could be somewhat hazardous:

"As you might know the New Zealand Strike Masters were fitted with an aircraft version on the GPMG (No butt, Electric firing solenoid and cocking stud instead of cocking handle). However there was 1 major difference. One gun (I can't remember which one) was opposite feed (The guns were mounted on their sides). This meant they had a different feed tray. A cam on the top of the bolt ran in a ramp in the bottom of the feed cover and drove the feed pawls feeding the ammunition. The problem that occurred was that occasionally the links would jam in the feed slot. This jammed the bolt at the start of the forward cycle. As soon as the feed cover was opened the cam was freed from the ramp

A Mk.88 of the RNZAF beating up the tower. (RNZAF Official, via Air Force Museum, Christchurch, NZ)

allowing the bolt to move forward, chamber and fire the round. There was no evidence left to what had actually occurred.

"I vaguely remember this happening during a test fire at the Butts (It was 30 years ago) The gun jammed, I lifted the feed cover and the gun fired. After a lot more puzzling a fix was worked out. On any gun stoppage on the aircraft the cocking cable was hooked on the cocking stud and the bolt was manually held back while the feed cover was opened and the stoppage cleared. All went well until 1 day the cocking lug (on the other side of the cocking stud and contacting the bolt) fractured. There was now nothing holding the bolt back and, you guessed it, we fired another round over the tarmac. After this no one walked in front of a Strikemaster until the armourers had done their thing!"

Paddy Kinloch, RNZAF Armourer.

The constant low level operation took its toll on the Mk.88, and by 1981 the aircraft were suffering advanced signs of fatigue. Areas around the fin and wing main structure were becoming seriously damaged due to the constant buffeting experienced at reduced altitude, and the fleet was consequently grounded in 1985 for repair. Six aircraft were re-winged whilst the others were carefully monitored with strain gauges and placed on reduced fatigue count operations. By 1988 the problem was getting worse, so much so that it affected the pilot training system that year and the next. It was clear that the Strikemaster would not last much longer without serious investment, and the New Zealand Government decided to initiate a search for a replacement. The following paragraph shows how the market had changed since those early pioneer days of the first jet trainers:

'The RNZAF is completing its evaluation of the ten tenders received for its BAe Strikemaster replacement programme, Project Falcon. The contenders are the Aermacchi MB.339, SIAI Marchetti S.211, British Aerospace Hawk, Casa C.101, Dassault-Breguet/ Dornier Alpha Jet, Embraer EMB.312 Tucano, FMA IA.63 Pampa, Hawker de Havilland PC-9, Pilatus PC-7, and the Shorts Tucano. The announcement of a final decision and contract signing has been delayed until the beginning of the new financial year as a cost-saving measure.'

Flight International, 25 March 1989, p. 31.

The first of the winning Aermacchi MB339s were handed over on 19 April 1991. By the end of the year there were more groundings of the Strikemaster fleet, as fatigue became apparent in other wing spar areas. The aircraft was officially retired on 17 December 1992, with a flying display held at Ohakea; incidentally, one of the pilots that day was an RAF exchange office S/L M.Longstaff. Six aircraft were retained by the RNZAF, four as instructional airframes and two making their way into museums. A further six were sold on in 1993, all but one making their way to Australia.

ECUADOR

The Ecuadorian Government ordered a total of sixteen aircraft for ground attack and COIN duties. The first batch of eight Mk.89s was delivered by sea in October 1972 and were subsequently stationed at Ulpiano Páez de Salinas. They were immediately pressed into service at the Ecuadorian School of Advanced Military Aviation 'Cosme Renella' where the first twenty-four students passed out in December; by the end of

The RNZAF used their Mk.88s for a number of tasks including target banner towing. (RNZAF Official, via Air Force Museum, Christchurch, NZ)

1973, courses had flown nearly 1,500 hours. Two aircraft were lost that year due to a heavy landing and an engine flame-out. In 1974 the squadron was disbanded and reformed at Taura as part of Squadron No.2313. Over the next four years 9,300 hours were amassed; however, four aircraft were lost to accidents. In 1976 a further eight aircraft, delivered in two batches replaced the losses of previous years.

On 27 January 1979 FAE255 suffered a flame-out whilst taking off from Taura; both aircrew ejected successfully, but a heavy landing caused one pilot to be paralysed. The reason for the engine failure was not discovered. On 23 November the same year FAE256 suffered a similar fate, again the cause of the malfunction was not discovered. This time the Commandant of the Air Force grounded all Strikemasters pending an investigation. This was, however, cut short, as in 1981 Ecuador went to war with neighbouring Peru. Squadron No. 2313 were reactivated and deployed to the border region near Guayaquil. On 14 October 1981 FAE243 suffered a flame-out again during take-off, both crew escaped, but once again the Strikemaster was

The Sudan had been expecting 10 new aircraft in 1983, however only three, including this, were delivered.

grounded. Conscious that sudden failures of equipment looked bad, BAe dispatched two engineers and a pilot to investigate the problem. Between May and June 1982 the team ran-flew-and ran again until 8 June the aircraft was declared safe. Unfortunately, a concerted search of the archive has failed to reveal the snag. The reason for BAe's sudden attentiveness can possibly be deduced by examining both the date and Ecuador's geographical position. On 2 April 1982 Argentinean forces made an amphibious assault on the Falkland Islands; two weeks earlier the Argentine flag had been flown at South Georgia. During the operation to restore the Islands to British sovereignty, the Conservative Government curried favour with as many South American countries as possible. It would appear that Ecuador was one of those.

Subsequently the aircraft were complemented with 6 Mk.90s from the last production run of the aircraft, by then at Hurn, during 1987/88. The aircraft had originally been destined for the Sudanese government; however, an arms embargo had prevented the delivery of all but three in 1983. Conflict broke out again in 1995 with the Cenepa War with Peru, and by 3 February Ecuadorian Strikemasters were in the thick of it, covering land operations and performing local ground attack missions. The type suffered further losses over the next decade including an airframe overstress in excess of 12g, a flame-out and a mid-air collision between two of a three ship formation on 20 April 1989. Surprisingly, in 2008 four aircraft, three Mk.89s and a single Mk.90 were still operated by 2313 in the light ground attack role. Even more surprisingly, Ecuador purchased ex-Botswana Air Force aircraft in 2006 presumably for spares recovery. However, one aircraft was later photographed in 2007 as FAE265 in a new red/black colour scheme, suggesting the type will remain in service in South America for some time yet.

WIND DOWN AND RESALE

By the mid-1970s the majority of Strikemaster operators were looking for a replacement. In many cases Soviet aircraft, often built under licence, were the aircraft of choice; however, a number still bought British. What is clear is that the aircraft, no matter how effective, was getting just too old. Higher performance aircraft were becoming available, often at a substantial subsidy or with other political incentives. Also, as neighbouring aircraft fleets were upgraded the Strikemaster became quite out-gunned, especially now a replacement was available.

'Strikemaster sales (about 130) may reach 150 eventually but orders are likely to be from already established customers. A new batch was laid down last year for this reason. The RAF is fully committed to the Hawk and export sales efforts by Hawker Siddeley are bound to cut across Strikemaster's future.'

Flight International, 22 May 1975, p. 827.

On 25 August 1980 the first of ten aircraft to be assembled and to fly from Hurn took off on a 1 hour 15 minute proving flight. G-16-26 was a Mk.90, destined for the Ecuadorian Air Force as replacement for one of their losses. This aircraft crashed in 2001. It had been manufactured as production line overspill, and was primarily aimed at the replacement market. However, amongst emerging nations and their low level defence procurement a trend was forming. BAe, like other manufacturers, saw that a refurbished fleet of light attack aircraft might well open the door to more

OJ9 a Mk.87 of the Botswana Defence Force after returning back to the UK. This aircraft was originally owned by Kenya.

An ex-Oman Mk.82 being readied for delivery to Singapore.

lucrative sales later on. This was effectively demonstrated when Kuwait and Kenya replaced their aircraft with Hawks. BAe took back all remaining Strikemaster aircraft, subsequently refurbishing them before a number were snapped up by Botswana. The Botswana Defence Force Air Wing was formed in 1977 in reaction to growing tensions and incursions into the country. In all nine Mk.83 and four Mk.87 aircraft were delivered. The first batch arrived in April 1988, and held the distinction of becoming the force's first jet powered aircraft. Strikemasters were used extensively in the COIN role. The aircraft remained in service until 1996, when the type was replaced by an order of Canadian CF-116s. Subsequently the aircraft were purchased by Global Aviation, who went on to disperse many of the airframes to the private sector. Two re-sales, however, are worthy of further expansion.

STRIKEMASTER FILMS LTD.

'"UK Fighter Jets Sold Into Ivory Coast War Zone"

'British Customs officials are to launch an inquiry into the sale of jet fighter which look likely to be involved in military operations against civilians and rebels in one of Africa's bloodiest civil wars. An Observer investigation has revealed a loophole allowing potentially lethal British military hardware to slip out of the country without official scrutiny, licence or control. The sale of the two Strikemaster jets to the Ivory Coast government discloses a trail which begins with a British air display pilot and ends with a former commando in the French special forces now plying his trade as a mercenary in the war-torn state.'

The Observer, Sunday June 29 2003. Antony Barnett, Public Affairs Editor.

It transpired that the two aircraft had originally been sold to a private British operator, who had flown them under civil registration at many airshows. Then in 2003 he had been approached by a businessman wishing to purchase the aircraft for a firm called 'Strikemaster Films Ltd.', who wanted them for work in South Africa. Subsequently one of the pair was discovered in the Ivory Coast, a region where civil war had been ongoing since 2002. The aircraft was identified by French peacekeepers who informed the government of Malta, from where the aircraft had been shipped. They searched the hangars at Safi and discovered a second aircraft ready for shipment. Interestingly, the exporter was found not guilty of supplying arms during an Embargo, because of the aircraft's civilian status:

'4. that evidence shows that the aircraft, the subject of these proceedings, was dismantled on the instructions of the accused and its component parts shipped to the Ivory Coast. Accused attests that while all the parts were exported they could not wholesome be reassembled to form an aircraft that could fly. Moreover there is sufficient evidence to show that the aircraft was registered as a civil aircraft and deemed to be so by the competent UK aviation authorities. The prosecution has not disproved this fact. Nor has the prosecution shown that the aircraft was armed or that it could possibly be turned into a combat/military aircraft. In this Court's opinion the fact that the aircraft was intended

Ivory Coast 'acquired two Strikemasters from a private owner in 2003, one was later destroyed by French Special Forces. This aircraft, wearing the RNZAF colours was photographed at Safi in Malta. © Roberto Benetti - www.flightlinemalta.com

to train Ivorian air force cadets is of no consequence and does not on its own translate the aircraft into a military one.'

Court Of Magistrates (Malta) As A Court Of Criminal Judicature. Magistrate Dr. Antonio Micallef Trigona.
Sitting of 10 January, 2008. Number 479/2007.

The fate of both aircraft is not clear. During an attack on the International Airport in November 2004, it was reported that French forces destroyed a Strikemaster whilst it was hangared. Later reports suggest a Strikemaster was flying reconnaissance missions as late as 2005, although this is, as yet, unconfirmed.

So, as we reach the end of the first decade of the twenty-first century, it looks like a handful of Strikemasters will prevail operationally. If we consider that the first aircraft were delivered to the Royal Saudi Air Force forty years ago, then that longevity is all the more impressive.

7.

Circuits and Bumps

Aircraft accidents are, thankfully, very infrequent. However, they do happen, and with a type like the Jet Provost culmatively clocking up thousands of hours a week, often piloted by well trained if inexperienced students, the odd prang could be seen as inevitable. We could survey any period over the life of the JP and present an accident list. However, the 1980s best demonstrate the multitude of occurrences that have brought about the demise of both aircraft and regrettably, on occasion, crew.

By the late 1970s the majority of Jet Provost bases were located in the north-east of Britain. In fact, most were ex-Royal Canadian Air Force stations and notorious for suffering bad weather; a number of crews had been lost on the North Yorkshire Moors as a direct result of it. Now, as training stations, they were totally at the mercy of such weather. I remember sitting in the line hut at Leeming for days on end due to fog and heavy rain. Naturally, the Jet Provost could operate in poor conditions if required; however, with student pilots it was considered to be better to sit it out. Unfortunately, this was not always a satisfactory situation, and, with a constant throughput of pilots, detachments were sometimes hastily organized. One such situation arose in early January 1981. With the prospect of persistent bad weather delaying the flying programme, a number of T.Mk.5As were detached from No.1 FTS Linton-on-Ouse to Leuchars on the east coast of Scotland. During the morning of 28 January a student pilot was briefed to fly a low-level navigation sortie from Leuchars to another airfield (undisclosed in the report), refuel and then return at high level. The following report extract describes the events following takeoff.

> 'The student pilot took off at midday from runway 27, climbed straight ahead as briefed, changed to the approach frequency at about 700ft. by manually dialing it and entered cloud at an estimated height of 1000ft. He requested and was given clearance to turn right onto a heading of 35°. He acknowledged this and the regional pressure settings. This was his last transmission. The aircraft was next seen exiting cloud in a near vertical descent; fractionally later another eyewitness saw the aircraft fly in the north easterly direction in a level flight attitude but banked to the right. Seconds later the aircraft crashed into a wheat field on the lower slopes of a hill, about one minute 43 seconds after take off. The student pilot made no attempt to eject and was killed instantly; the aircraft was destroyed.'

'Aircraft Accident involving the Royal Air Force Jet Provost T5A XW308.'
Military aircraft accident summaries: MAAS 3/82. 10 February 1982.

XM364 Belly landing at Syerston 11 February 1960 (Crown)

Unfortunately, the nature of the accident could not be determined; however, it was considered likely that while the pilot altered his heading, the aircraft entered a steep spiral dive, and the pilot possibly blacked out under the G. forces exerted as he tried to correct the loss of height. He was clearly conscious in the last few seconds of flight as he was trying to recover from the dive; unfortunately, he was too late and too low.

BIRDSTRIKES

As any aircraft operator or pilot knows, one of the most hazardous situations can be caused by the smallest of birds hitting the airframe or being ingested by the engine. Naturally, Jet Provosts have encountered many such situations, and a number are described here. The control and removal of birds from airfields takes many forms. Techniques can range from loud bangs using thunder flashes through to captive Hawks and Owls; even the length of the grass can have an effect on numbers. Unfortunately, not all incidents involving birds are within the boundaries of the airfield, nor are they always as straightforward as one would imagine.

In the early 1980s a number of airfields in the eastern region were kept operational as part of the flight training programme. Naturally, trainee pilots undertake hundreds of circuits and landings while on their courses. With several stations operating the Jet Provost in close proximity, it was deemed prudent to use these extra fields to relieve pressure and give experience of other stations.

On 31 July 1980 a T.Mk.3A from RAF Church Fenton was practicing circuits and landings at RAF Elvington, near York. While climbing away from a roller at around 140kt, the pilot saw a large flock of birds directly ahead. Unable to take avoiding action, he passed through it, immediately losing engine power. With no possibility of turning back onto the runway the pilot turned towards open ground and ejected, suffering back injuries. The subsequent investigation noted that two birds had passed down the intake, blanking off nearly 40% of the total engine compressor and causing a flame-out. The origin of the birds was unusual:

> 'It transpired that some 500 racing pigeons had been released 10 miles to the south of the airfield with an intended destination that was likely to lead them to overfly the airfield at the time of the accident. However, the code of practice for pigeon fanciers that existed at the time did not require the release to be notified to that airfield and so neither the pilot nor the controllers at the airfield were aware of the potential dangers.'

'Aircraft Accident Involving Royal Air Force Jet Provost T3 XN590.'
Military Aircraft Accident Summaries MAAS 5/82 19 February 1982.

The incident resulted in the RAF and Royal Pigeon Racing Association, who already co-operated at a national level, re-evaluating communication between local clubs and neighbouring airfields. The forestry commission was compensated £1,000 for damage to trees; no claim was made for the birds.

On 15 August 1984 Jet Provost T.Mk.3A XN473 took off from Cranwell on a medium level navigation exercise. As the aircraft became airborne, the QFI saw a large flock of small birds dead ahead. He pulled back on the stick in an attempt to climb over them; however, it rapidly became clear that his rate of ascent was not enough. The only course of action left open to him was to abandon the takeoff, and he closed the throttle and lowered the nose preparing the aircraft to land on the remaining runway. Unfortunately, the rate of descent was such that the aircraft hit the runway heavily, collapsing the nose undercarriage leg and bursting both main wheel tyres.

> 'The presence of the flock of birds was the single most important factor contributing to the accident. The instructor was faced with a possible bird strike and engine failure in a position from which neither an abandoned takeoff nor an ejection could have been accomplished safely. He therefore correctly chose to abandon the takeoff before he struck the birds and whilst sufficient runway was remaining ahead of him. However, his subsequent decision to close the throttle when the aircraft was at a very low airspeed committed the aircraft to an excessively heavy landing.'

'Aircraft Accident involving the Royal Air Force Jet Provost T3A XN473.'
Military aircraft accident summaries: MAAS 9/85. 14 May 1985.

Both crewmembers survived the incident with no more than a reprimand; unfortunately, the aircraft was cat. 5, and that was without actually hitting the birds. Just nine months earlier a Leeming aircraft I was familiar with was struck by several birds while on a low-level sortie. This time one of the crew was very lucky to escape:

> 'The instructor immediately took control from the student and initiated a climbing turn towards his base airfield. Although the throttle had not been moved there was a marked loss of thrust from the engine combined with an unusual rumbling noise. When the aircraft was in a glide descent from 1500 ft, it was noticed that the jet pipe temperature was in excess of 800° C. There was insufficient height left to enable completion of the drills as appropriate to the apparent engine surge so the instructor, having transmitted distress calls, ordered abandonment as the aircraft approached high ground. The student

Above and below: No.7 FTS, Church Fenton on 29/1/63. Collided whilst landing on the same runway in poor visibility.

was unhurt but the instructor sustained a compression fracture of the spine. The aircraft crashed near the top of the small moorland hill, bursting into flames an impact.'

'Aircraft Accident involving the Royal Air Force Jet Provost T3A XM453.'
Military aircraft accident summaries: MAAS 17/84. 26 September 1984.

STUDENTS

Naturally, a student flying solo for the first time is a stressful event; however, it is on subsequent missions that problems can be encountered. Usually the briefing ensures all eventualities are catered for, but, however well prepared the student and however confident the QFI in his abilities, sometimes accidents still happen. What follows are just a few examples involving Jet Provosts.

On a bright clear July day in 1981 a student pilot in the early stages of training was briefed on flying a general handling sortie, to include some rudimentary aerobatics. In No.11 Low Flying Zone (Vale of Pickering) he climbed to 9000ft and proceeded to execute a number of stall turns. Half way through a further turn the engine flamed out. An attempted relight was unsuccessful and the student made an emergency call on the distress frequency. Only the carrier wave was received, as a radio malfunction prevented the voice signal.

'The student became so preoccupied with the radio problem making various switch selections, that he was unable to make a further attempt to restart the engine and realized only just in time that he would have to eject.'

He managed to point the aircraft at open fields before successfully ejecting at around 1000ft. The board determined that he mishandled the aircraft during the final manoeuvre causing the engine to flame-out. The engine did not relight, owing to the disturbed airflow into the engine. The following comments demonstrate the situation a student can find himself in:

'On this occasion a young pilot in the early stage of training was trying hard to improve his skill at aerobatics when he experienced an engine malfunction. Although he had been briefed on engine failures and had simulated them he would, nevertheless, have been under a great deal of stress – the more so as he experienced a radio problem as well.'

'Aircraft Accident Involving Royal Air Force Jet Provost T3A XN643.'
Military Aircraft Accident Summaries MAAS 2/83 8 February 1983.

On the afternoon of 9 December 1982, T.Mk.5A XW417 formed part of a four stream from RAF Church Fenton on a low-level navigation exercise. Aircraft one, two and four deviated around low cloud and poor visibility in an area of high ground; XW417 did not.

'Witnesses saw XW417 manoeuvring at low-level, in poor weather conditions over Lake Thirlmere, some 3nms west of its intended course. The aircraft was next seen descending out of the mist in a very steep nose down attitude at high speed and it crashed into fir trees close to the side of the lake. The resulting fireball was seen by numerous witnesses.'

'Aircraft Accident Involving Royal Air Force Jet Provost T5A XW417.'
Military Aircraft Accident Summaries MAAS 13/84 4 April 1984.

The board of enquiry considered that the student probably became disorientated in cloud and as a result lost control of the aircraft.

On 11 May 1984 a student was returning to No.1 FTS at RAF Linton-on-Ouse. On his approach another Jet Provost was seen on the runway forcing him to abort the landing and return into circuit.

An unidentified aircraft at Syerston 12 November 1965. The aircraft was clearly scrap after the event.

'His subsequent circuit and final approach were seen to be erratically flown, culminating in a late touch down to the left of the runway centre line, and with insufficient allowance for the crosswind that was present. The aircraft bounced and continued to drift left with the student applying full brake as he realized his proximity to the far end of the runway. Towards the latter part of the landing both tyres burst and, after slewing right and then left, the aircraft engaged the arrestor barrier. Because the aircraft was displaced from the centre line, the left wing suffered extensive damage when it struck the port barrier stanchion.'

Aircraft Accident Involving Royal Air Force Jet Provost T3A XN641.
Military Aircraft Accident Summaries MAAS 6/85/2 24 April 1985.

It subsequently transpired that at the pre-flight brief the QFI had stated a minimum fuel load and the student had reached this point during the second approach. Normally a poor approach would be aborted and another circuit flown, however the student, distracted by the fuel content, pressed home the landing. Unfortunately he touched down late and was heavy on the brakes, exacerbated by a strong crosswind, however he continued with his flying training after the event.

QFIs

And its not just student pilots that get it wrong sometimes, on occasion the Qualified Flying Instructor (QFI) could find himself in an awkward position.

'On 6 June 1986, a pair of Jet Provost aircraft were engaged in a tail chase, an exercise in which one aircraft follows the other through a series of manoeuvres at a safe distance. For approximately 5 minutes the second aircraft maintain position, with normal variations in range and lateral displacement, until the leader pulled up into a wing-over to the left. During the wing-over the leader lowered flap, tightened the turn and, on rolling wings level in the descent, looked behind unsuccessfully for the number 2 aircraft. After some three seconds he looked ahead and saw it head-on at a range of 200-300m. At the start of the wing-over the number 2 had been laterally displaced in the leader's eight o'clock position - and saw the leader fly a tight wing-over to the left, ending up head-on at close range. Their attempts at avoiding one another were unsuccessful and the leaders aircraft passed over the No.2 aircraft, striking the rear fuselage and shearing off its entire tail assembly. Both aircraft descended out of control and the three occupants ejected successfully. Both aircraft were destroyed.'

'Aircraft Accident Involving Royal Air Force Jet Provost T5A XW407 & XW411.' Military Aircraft Accident Summaries MAAS 1/87 9 February 1987.

In that instance the board decided on both evidence and testimonies that both pilots had failed to take timely or corrective avoiding action, leading to the loss of both aircraft, all three occupants ejected safely. But not everything is down to the man at the controls and on occasion a technical malfunction has been the cause of lost aircraft.

On 22 October 1981 a T.Mk.3A, XM366 from Church Fenton, encountered an engine malfunction after executing a stall turn. A hot relight was unsuccessful and the pilot elected to land at the nearest airfield, on this occasion Holme-upon-Spalding Moor. Unfortunately the aircraft was too shallow in its approach to make a forced landing and the pilot ejected, the aircraft was destroyed. When the engine was removed and inspected by the manufacturer two separate defects were discovered. The fuel control system was contaminated and the atomizers within the engine were partially blocked with carbon deposits. This dictated that no matter how hard the pilot had tried the engine would never have relit. Engine inspection schedules were changed in light of this accident.

Six months later a T.Mk.4, XP564 from RAF Brawdy crashed into the reservoir at Nant-Y-Moch after the pilots experienced a throttle restriction and were unable to increase the engine RPM above 50%. Once the aircraft had been recovered and inspected it was discovered that the throttle cable had failed on the students (starboard) side. As both pilots and students throttles are connected by the same continuous cable loop, the failure rendered both inoperative. The failure of the cable was due to the fact it had been incorrectly fitted, instead of being routed around the pulley it was around the guard. Through repeated use the cable had eventually snapped causing loss of the aircraft.

However, the causes of some incidents were, despite the best efforts of the Air Accident Board investigations, destined to remain a mystery.

On the afternoon of 17 May 1982 a T.Mk.5A took off from Linton-on-Ouse to carry out a display practice for the forthcoming Wright Jubilee Trophy aerobatic competition. Due to a low cloud base it was decided that one manoeuvre, a vertical role, should be changed to a loop, avoiding the cloud.

'Towards the end of the display the pilot entered a barrel roll to the left; the first part of the manoeuvre was well flown but as the aircraft reached the inverted position at the apex of the manoeuvre the rate of role slowed down and the rate of pitch increased.

Above and below: Unidentified aircraft with collapsed U/C note lifting hoist.

The aircraft assumed a near vertical nose-down attitude, heading some 90 degrees off the intended display line. The pilot attempted to pull the aircraft out of the dive but was unsuccessful and it struck the ground inside the airfield perimeter in a flat, slightly nose down attitude at high speed.'

'Aircraft Accident Involving Royal Air Force Jet Provost T5A XW288.'
Military Aircraft Accident Summaries MAAS 20/83 12 July 1983.

903 Strikemaster Mk.80, 'pancaked' after a flat spin.

After hitting the ground the aircraft skidded across the concrete apron and struck the end of one of Linton's hangars, forcing the heavy door open and demolished part of Engineering Records located in the brick built annex. It also narrowly missed personnel nearby and destroyed a motor cycle; the motor cycle owner was subsequently compensated. The cause of the accident remains unknown.

CIVILIAN

Accidents are not the preserve of the military, incidents both here and abroad have beset civilian registered types in the last few years. Interestingly a number are related specifically to issues surrounding the ejection seats and demonstrate some of the extra dimensions operating ex-military on civil registers brings.

There have been a number of fatalities since Jet Provosts started to appear on the civil list. On 24 December 1998 the pilot of G-BWBS a T.Mk.5A came down in the sea just a mile from Bradwell-on-Sea, Essex. The pilot successfully ejected. Tragically he did not survive his time in the sea. The Board considered if he had been wearing a life jacket he might well have survived. A further two crew members lost their lives in a low-level accident close to the River Severn on 1 August 1999. G-TOMG a rare T.Mk.4 was destroyed on impact.

On 12 February 2001 Jet Provost T.Mk.5A G-BYED was returning from a short flight around the Londonderry, visibility was good and there was no significant weather. Turning into the circuit at around 700ft the engine ran down.

'The pilot transmitted a mayday call to the tower, retracted the flaps and without an active ejector seat had no option but to select a suitable area on which to carry out a forced landing. The only area available to him was the mud flats of the Loch Foyle estury. He decided to retract the landing gear and carried out a successful forced landing touching down at an estimated 80kt to 90kt. The touchdown caused only minimal damage to the underside of the fuselage.'

AAIB Bulletin No: Ref:EW/G2001/02/06

The pilot was almost immediately rescued by a British Army Helicopter, the aircraft was recovered by Chinook after it had been partially submerged by a number of tides. The aircraft indicated 800lbs of fuel on board at the time of the incident, engineers consider the HP fuel pump drive shaft sheared starving the engine of fuel.

On 18 August 2002 a T.Mk.3A G-BVEZ took off from Humberside Airport and very nearly did not return:-

'The aircraft was carrying out a flight test with both the pilot and an observer using oxygen supplied by the aircraft's integral oxygen system. On climbing through FL240, the pilot became unconscious due to a disconnection in his oxygen hose at the break point with his ejection seat. The ejection seats had been deactivated and were not equipped with their emergency oxygen bottles. The observer managed to control the aircraft, descending it sufficiently for the pilot to regain consciousness and subsequently to return to their departure airfield for a normal landing.'

AAIB Bulletin No. 8/2003. Ref. EW/C2002/08/04

The upper main spar attachment lug damage from the Australian crash on 5 October 2006. (Australian Transport Safety Bureau Ref. Nov2007/DOTARS 50390)

However, it is from Australia that the accident that might yet see aircraft grounded happened in 2006.

Abstract

At about 1215 Eastern Standard Time on 5 October 2006, the pilot of a British Aircraft Corporation 167 Strikemaster aircraft took off from Bathurst, NSW, for a 25-minute joy flight with one passenger. The flight was intended to include high-level aerobatics followed by a low-level simulated strike mission. When the aircraft failed to return, a search was initiated and the aircraft wreckage was located in the Turon State Forest about 20Km to the NE of Bathurst. The ground impact started a fuel-fed fire that resulted in a large bushfire, which took several days to contain. The pilot and passenger were fatally injured.

Australian Transport Safety Bureau Ref. Nov2007/DOTARS 50390

On investigation it was discovered that the aircraft had broken up before it hit the ground. The starboard wing had separated from the aircraft after a period of downward bending fracturing the upper main spar attachment lug. Both horizontal stabilizers were ripped from the aircraft in an upward motion and the rudder detached about the same time. It appears that the spar had had work done sometime previously which may have contributed to the accident. Whatever the cause the findings were distributed in both Australia and the United Kingdom. It appears flight restrictions might well be on the way.

Notwithstanding those accidents noted the Jet Provost has proved to be an extremely safe aircraft. The number of hours and 'student punishment' that they have suffered over the years has demonstrated its resilience to damage. Unfortunately by the early 1980s the aircraft was getting a little long in the tooth. Fatigue had already claimed most of the T.Mk.4s by the mid-1970s and it was recognized that the rest of the fleet would need serious structural work at the current use of airframe life, possibly by the mid-1980s. The side-by-side cockpit arrangement, whilst popular with many instructors, no longer prepared the student for the next phase of training. And at £60,000 per aircraft/year the operating costs, especially that linked with fuel, was becoming totally uneconomic. The problem was what do you replace a Jet Provost with other than another Jet Provost?

8.

'They are going to find it quite a handful initially'

On 18 June 1984 the Government issued an invitation to tender against Air Staff Target (AST) 412, the Jet Provosts service days were now numbered. The planning of a replacement of the aircraft had been proposed much earlier, however the type of propulsion, cockpit layout and even whether to buy British or not rolled on for the better part of the 1980s. In this section we look into who wanted what and the surprising reason for a Brazilian aircraft being built in Northern Ireland.

CONTENDERS

It was clear by the early 1980s that someone was going to have to decide whether to re-wing the Jet Provost fleet or replace it with something more appropriate. Kevin McNamara, MP for Hull North, raised the issue in the Commons during a debate on the RAF's role in Falklands Conflict.

'I understand that discussions are going on at official level. The RAF is talking about its needs, and the industry is looking at what it can supply. I know, too, that the advanced stage of the P110 has not yet been reached. However, in my view, it is something that we shall need in the future, and we should do better to think in terms of using a jet trainer that is British manufactured, instead of being forced, perhaps at the last minute when the Jet Provosts are so clapped out that they cannot be used again, to get something quickly from the Italians or the United States. We should do better to consider the matter at this stage.

'What will be our basic trainer to succeed the Jet Provost? Some say that we should use a light, unsophisticated aircraft such as the Bulldog. Others say that we should use an aeroplane such as the P164, which I believe to be too similar to the Hawk for basic and subsequent training. We must find a basic trainer in the near future. A host of questions must still be answered. Do we want a tandem trainer or a side-by-side trainer? Instructors cannot come to a unanimous view. Time is not on our side.'

House of Commons Debate, 22 July 1982, vol 28 cc566-626.

Naturally, McNamara had the interests of his constituency at heart. The BAe factory at Brough had been constructing the Hawk for some time and he was confident two local projects, P110 and P164, were essential for the RAF. The P110 can be best described as a fore-runner to the Typhoon whilst the P164 was a lower order version of the Hawk. Both were proposed as a 'package' for the services – neither were built. McNamara's comments were, however, true. At the rate aircraft were flying it was probable that most of the Jet Provost fleet, even with careful management of fatigue, would indeed be 'clapped out' by the mid-1980s. The increase in the requirement for fast jet pilots, driven especially by both GR1 and ADV F3 Tornado squadrons forming, had seen to that.

As with any military contract, competition was expected to be fierce. The aviation world had radically changed since the days of Percival's first jet powered P.84. The attraction of low cost – large volume contracts for training aircraft, however remained just the same. So when AST 412 was issued in July 1983 the Government was a little taken aback by the initial response and where they originated.

'*Miles is back! Miles, famous for such trainers as the Magister, Master, and Martinet, is to re-enter the trainer world with a bid for the Royal Air Force Jet Provost basic trainer replacement*'. ran the *Flight International* headline in August 1983. Unfortunately their proposal was no more than a re-hash of the M-100 Student the company had proposed and flown in hope of displacing the initial Jet Provost order. Miles suggested a tandem cockpit, similar to the Hawk, new engine, uprated avionics and fuel system and extensive use of composite materials. In all the 'new Miles Merlin' would incorporate around 55% of the original aircraft. '*Flight understands that Miles would welcome formal partnership on the Merlin project from aviation engineering companies.*' It is not clear whether any enquiries were made, however the aircraft never left the drawing board.

The Pilatus PC-9 front runner and sore loser.(Photograph by Adrian Pingstone)

The amount of interest from outside the United Kingdom was staggering. Designs flooded in from around the world encompassing a mix of major and minor companies including Aerospatiale, Australian Aircraft Consortium, Beech/Eagle Aircraft Services, Caproni Vizzola/Charlotte Aircraft, Casa, DK Aviation, Embraer/CSE Aviation, Fairchild/Garrett Air Research, Pilatus/Britten-Norman, Rhein-Flugzeugbau and Siai Marchetti. What was immediately apparent from the contenders was who was serious and who was speculative. A number of foreign manufacturers had already formed consortiums with British companies as it was clear that whoever eventually won the contract would have to build the aircraft in the UK. A number of other British firms expressed an interest including Edgeley Aircraft with a turbo-shaft powered design utilising lessons learned from the Optica, British Aerospace with two variants' of the P164 and Firecracker Aircraft, a company formed specifically to tender for the contract.

Throughout the winter of 1983-84 all designs were scrutinised against AST 412. A budgetary and technical analysis allowed the proposals to be divided into three broad groups: Jet; high performance propeller; and low performance propeller. Air Staff Target 412 was far-reaching. It called for at least 155 aircraft that could be powered by turboprop or turbofan. It had to incorporate a cockpit not too dissimilar from the Hawk. The aircraft should be capable of climbing to 15,000ft in 7min from 'brakes off' and be capable of a 25,000ft service ceiling. Speed should encompass 270kt (CAS); 210kt at sea level during maximum continuous power and power off stall speed of just 60kt. Take-off should be attained at maximum all up weight in no more than 2,000ft on a prepared surface, preferably up to a 30kt cross-wind. The undercarriage should be able to withstand a 13ft/per second landing (essential for a training aircraft) and the airframe should be able to withstand and airframe load of +6g/-3g. The figures supplied, with consideration of through life costs, allowed the MOD to cut the field down to just four contenders; the Swiss Pilatus PC9; Brazilian Tucano; Australian Wamira and the home grown Firecracker. All except the Wamira were in an advanced stage of development at the time of the announcement.

FIREWORKS!

Central to any order being placed with a foreign manufacturer was the amount of off-set that could be gained by reciprocal orders. Basically if we buy from you you must buy from us. The process also dictated how much work could be undertaken in the purchasers country and required comparable size of orders. Clearly, the process was extremely restrictive and, if sufficient caution was not exercised, could see the United Kingdom loosing out. To put this into context; ordering the Swiss airframe relied heavily on their reciprocal order for Hawks. Unfortunately past dealings had not worked out as was initially hoped. By 1984 Britain had sold 350 aircraft to Switzerland, a great many of them Hunters, only 25% had been fitted out in the UK, the rest built under licence. To make matters worse the country had also recently purchased Rapier – these were all to be built in Swiss factories. And building in Swiss factories meant a lack of British jobs, a situation not missed by the opposition.

The Australian proposal was no more than a 'paper aircraft', not expected to fly until 1986 at the earliest. This meant that if the aircraft was chosen the British Government would be funding up to three years worth of development. Clearly, if this was the case then the projects proposed by British manufacturers would be a better return. The Tucano, proposed by the Brazilian manufacturer Embraer, had more potential but problems in other areas. In its favour was the fact that the manufacturer had signed a deal with Short Brothers in Belfast that allowed for the complete construction of

130 of the aircraft in Northern Ireland, only 25 were to be built in Brazil. On the downside; at the time Brazil had the third largest balance of payments deficit in the world and it was hard to see how they would be able to provide an off-set that the UK Government didn't indirectly pay for. There was also the problem of Britain's political appearance in South America so soon after the Falklands conflict.

As far as many were concerned the race to provide the RAF with a successor to the Jet Provost was a one horse race:

> 'The Hunting Firecracker will be built by the Hunting Group of Companies, which is one of the leading defence contractors in this country. This group built the Jet Provost, currently in service, the Piston Provost and the Percival Prentice. Huntings have a record of 40 years of providing training aircraft for the Royal Air Force and for export markets and the product support for these activities. The foreign aircraft, the Tucano and the Pilatus PC9, are surrounded by hypothetical offset and counter-trade deals that are more complicated than an Agatha Christie novel. None of the offset deals is tangible and all are likely to be pie in the sky.'

The Earl of Kimberley, House of Lords Debate, 17 October 1984, vol. 455 cc1056-73.

On 21 March 1985, Michael Heseltine, Secretary for State for Defence announced in Parliament that the new training aircraft for the RAF was to be the Tucano. The Firecracker and Wamira were rejected on their submitted bid price bringing the competition down to just two aircraft. Both the Tucano and PC-9 had easily met the RAFs required specification and so the two had been judged on cost alone, unofficially Officers suggested the would be *'no violent opposition to Tucano'*. The Embraer – Shorts project would cost the British tax payer £125 million a whopping £60 million less than the Swiss designed PC-9, more importantly the contract would reinvigorate Northern Ireland. The Troubles had ensured that very little investment

RAF Church Fenton presided over the switch to turboprop training. (Courtesy MOD)

had been forthcoming since the start of the 1960s, whilst traditional industries such as shipbuilding had been in steady decline. It was now possible that over 600 engineering jobs could be created, at least filling the gap left by the failure of the DeLorean car manufacturer in late 1982. Further, and more importantly, Shorts would be able to increase the number of young people currently employed on apprenticeships to nearly 130 per year, an important factor in the 'battle for hearts and minds' the Government was currently waging in the Province.

Naturally, there were those who cried foul. Kevin McNamara who had fought the British Aerospace corner, accused the Government of making Shorts a more attractive investment opportunity (the firm was going to be privatised in the near future) and *'for settling the odd debt with Brazil'* (in return for emergency landing rights during the Falklands War). There was also a salutary assessment of the bidding process and outcome published in *'Flight International'* that is worth repeating here:

> 'And some Officers, Flight understands, are 'not sure that the powers that be appreciate the bashing that the engine will get in the training environment. Students don't handle engines like airline pilots do, and the Garrett was designed for high level cruising, not for the sort of thrashing that the students will give it'.

The first students to *'thrash'* the aircraft were those on Basic Flying Course 42 at Church Fenton from December 1989. Shorts were contracted to deliver 35 aircraft per year, building a fleet of 130 by 1992. Interestingly the MOD intended to start disposing of Jet Provosts from the mid-1990s and keep a few on, in the navigation and TWU roles until at least the turn of the century. Alas it was not to be. As the first Tucano equipped course started at No.7 FTS RAF Church Fenton world changing events were being played out across Central Europe.

As 1989 played out, Soviet control over the Central European states was slowly relaxed. Poland and Hungary were the first to move towards more self-governance, and by November East Germany had reached boiling point. In Leipzig on the 5 October, the day after Gorbachev announced that reforms were needed in the East German state if it were to survive, 100,000 marched calling for free election. Eric Honecker, head of the GDR, ordered state police to open fire – they refused, setting in motion the single most defining moment of the later 20th Century. On the night of the 9 November 1989 the border between East and West Berlin was opened and by 25 December 1991 the Soviet Union itself had gone.

The British government moved swiftly. Through the language of review swingeing defence cuts were made as first *'Options for Change'* (25 July 1990) and the *'Peace Dividend'* and was swiftly replaced by the *'Defence Costs Study"* (1994) encompassing *'Front Line First'*. The RAF was almost halved in strength though the 1990s as major stations closed including a number of those with flying training commitments. Any chance of the Jet Provost remaining in service, by 1990 one aircraft was costing £70,000 per year to operate, was now scuppered. The last course on Jet Provosts graduated from No.1 FTS RAF Linton-on-Ouse on 4 July 1993. The last Jet Provost left service from No.6 FTS RAF Finningley later that year ending the 'all through' jet training experiment that had started at No.2 FTS 29 years earlier.

From then on disposal became fairly arbitrary. The majority flew to RAF Shawbury awaiting disposal, however a number of higher fatigue airframes were scrapped on site. Between March 1990 and March 1994 115 aircraft had been sold, by competitive tender, private treaty and public auction (the first being held by Phillips on 8 July 1993) to twenty customers, the receipts for those sales totalled £600,000. A further 62 were disposed of in 1994/5, along with 87 Viper engines and 10 Trollyaccs. The sales paved the way for the current phase of the Jet Provost story – the private fleet.

T.Mk.3s & 5s are regular visitors to British and European air shows

Private Strikemaster at Kemble 2005

This Jet Provost at the museum Boscombe Down, was used as an apprentice training aid for 10 years. It is now awaiting refurbishment to display standard.

The future of RAF Flying Training currently rests with the Short Tucano. It is unlikely the aircraft will have the same longevity as the Jet Provost. (Courtesy MOD)

Members of the public now had the chance to own a light-jet aircraft with a military history, demonstrating how popular the aircraft was, many stepped forward.

Clearly not everyone lamented the passing of the aircraft as this published letter points out:

> 'The RAF is about to retire its Hunting/Percival/BAC/BAe/UncleTom-Cobbley Jet Provosts. In celebration of this grand gesture to environmentalism, it even arranged a fly past of 14 of them at Linton-on-Ouse (which has now got one as a gate-guardian, too). The press release speaks of the lesser orange-tailed thunder brick as being "...held in the same high esteem and affection as other such long-servers as the Hunter and the Canberra." Not by the poor blighters who've lived near 38 years worth of constant-thrust, variable noise thump-and-staggers, it 'aint, Mate. To say nothing of what the local residents think...'

Flight International, 26 May-1 June 1993.

SURVIVORS

Current estimations put around sixty aircraft in flying condition, with a number under restoration as I speak. The only mark not represented is the T.Mk.2, which is unsurprising as only four were built. The flying examples range the T.Mk.1 currently operated by Kennet Aviation at North Weald, originally G-AOBU now under the serial XD693. Eleven T.Mk.3s spread across Britain, the USA and South Africa, Four T.Mk.4s of which three are in the UK and a further model in Puerto Rico. Twenty-

four T.Mk.5s and a further 21 Strikemasters are currently in flying condition, within these are the four still operated by the Ecuadorian Air Force. And when we add to this the number currently in museums, training establishments (both military and civil), private collections, gate guards and even some in enthusiasts gardens, including one T.51 actually in a children's playground in Sri Lanka, that number jumps by at least a further 182, granted some of these are no more than cockpits or other large pieces of fuselage, but the point is nearly one third of the total aircraft built still survive! This makes an encounter with a Jet Provost at a museum or airshow extremely likely. And whether it is in the air or on the ground I hope this book will help you to appreciate what a big part this little plane has played British aviation history both at home and abroad.

APPENDIX ONE
Jet Provost Trials Unit
(Far East)

The personal recollections courtesy of Mick Ryan first CO of the trials Unit from August to December 1965.

The following account gives a vivid insight into the type of the trials work undertaken by the Jet Provost. It also describes some of the conditions that the Royal Air Force were operating in during the 1960s. Due to the unusual nature of the work reported by Mick Ryan, Commanding Officer of the first round of trials, I have decided to present them here with only minor modifications.

The trial was mounted during the height of the Indonesian Crisis in the last six months of 1965. There were Hunter and Canberra squadrons in Malaysia and Singapore but the UK had very little experience of using Forward Air Control in jungle terrain. Most of our experience had been in Europe or the Middle East. A 250ft tree canopy presented a new challenge if air support was to be employed effectively in Central Malaysia and Borneo.

The Chief Scientist's Department, led by Don Spiers, initiated a trial to examine the best way to bring in air support from the ground in jungle terrain. In early July 1965 calls were advertised for volunteers to man the trials unit which intended to use three Jet Provost Mk.4s.

I had done one 2½-year tour on Hunter F.6s on 93 Sqn at RAF Jever in Germany and then completed a QFI course in 1961. After 2 years instructing on JPs at Cranwell, and ignoring the advice of my betters, I took my A2 QFI test and ended up back on the staff of CFS teaching QFIs on the JPs 3 and 4. Still not listening properly, I was one of the first "waterfront" staff to take my A1 after a two year sulk between the "waterfront" and the "Trappers". I was all lined up to go on exchange to the Royal Australian Air Force at Sale at the end of my tour. I'd sold my car learnt "Oz" from my next door neighbour when, to everyone's surprise, I was promoted to Sqn Ldr on 1 July 1965. I quickly volunteered for the trial hoping this might be a way back on to operational flying. I had about 1,100 JP hours at the time. MoD was surprised when the QFI for the trial turned out to be a Sqn Ldr but, after some muttering, they allowed me to Command the unit.

A frantic two months followed in the UK whilst it was arranged for three new Jet Provost Mk.4s, XS221, XS223 and XS224, to be dismantled and flown out to Singapore in three Argosys. This was a first for the RAF as we had never taken a JP apart before but there was no way we could have flown them out.

At the same time I was joined by Roy Holmes, Hunter QFI from Chivenor OCU and Bob Innes a South African JP QFI who had some ground attack experience. Later we

163

Jet Provost T.Mk.4 showing the detachment badge. (Mick Ryan)

were to be joined in Singapore by Sqn Ldr George Ord, an experienced Hunter ground attack operator.

There was a lot of early research into the possibilities of flying the JPs from Malaysia to Borneo – 400+ nm. Close to the limit of the JP and also pushing the limits for aircrew for long cold soaks at high altitude. The aircraft were dismantled, loaded into their Argosys and flown out to Changi in early August. The engineers wrote themselves a dismantling schedule and also an Erection Schedule (sounds disgusting!) – but more of that later. The wings, tailfin and elevators were removed and with tilting blocks the fuselage just fitted into the Argosy. The three pilots flew out to Singapore by Comet on Sunday 15th August 1965.

We installed ourselves with 20 Sqn Hunters, at Tengah and the three JPs were moved to Seletar for assembly. Then the troubles started. Someone in the supply chain had thought it a good idea to off-load the boxes with all our Erection Schedules and some critical bolts. We had flown out our own volunteer ground crew and Chief Tech Baker was a brilliant lead. Fortunately, being a nit-picking QFI, I had brought out my own Technical Volume 1 for the Mk.4; none of the other documents had arrived. We cursed the supply chain but we had to acknowledge there was a war on in both Borneo and up country in Malaysia! Chiefy Baker, with some help from the engineers at Seletar, used my Vol 1 and the Dismantling Schedule, which had very usefully been kept with the airframes, to write themselves an Erection Schedule – which they dutifully followed. For the first time the RAF assembled its own JPs.

Unfortunately there was some missing vital tail bolts and someone had damaged one of the airframes with a screwdriver. We also had no trestles upon which to assemble the airframes. After frantic signals back to UK and scouring the airfields in Singapore, we managed to solve all the problems and the first aircraft XS224 was ready for air test on Saturday 28th August – only 14 days after arrival in theatre. I got airborne at 14:09 and after an almost perfect air test lasting 1:40, landed at Tengah. The engine acceleration times were slightly slow and the DME aerials had been connected up in reverse, both snags that were easily fixed.

Assembling the T.Mk.4s – without the aid of a full AP set! (Mick Ryan)

That was the least of my problems. We were to be operating out of a Kidde Inflatable Hangar on 20 Sqn's dispersal at Tengah. That Saturday afternoon was the Squadron party to celebrate 20 Sqn's 50th birthday. On taxying in I was immediately surrounded by a wildly cheering and a very happy bunch of airmen who would not let me out of the cockpit until I had drunk a considerable quantity of Tiger beer. My first time drunk in charge of an aircraft.

Having staggered out of the cockpit, I was horrified to see them enthusiastically push my first precious JP off the edge of the concrete and up to its axle in soft mud. Don't worry they said with great confidence and about twenty of them got under the wing and lifted the wheel back onto the concrete. They thought my "kiddie car" was a great toy after their Hunters!. A quick hose down and they pushed it into the inflatable hangar with no damage. I'm glad Chiefy Baker was not there to see it. 20 Squadron under the CO Max Bacon, were great hosts and we operated very happily out of their facilities for the first six weeks. We quickly got the other two JPs assembled and operational.

The trial was run under the stewardship of Don Spiers in London, Gilbert Hoare the charming FEAF Command Scientist and attached to the unit was a young scientist Roger Noades. Roger was the brains behind our outfit. He set our flying targets and the balance of dual and solo, airspeeds and heights which were all taped on special Hussenot recorders mounted in the rear fuselage. We pressed a button on the control column at critical points on the test, e.g. Start of run, overhead IP, contact with the target and then we had to bring back gun camera film of the target taken from a realistic diving attack.

We had some slightly different equipment on our JP4s. I have mentioned the recorders and we also had gun sights and GR.90 gun cameras. All these needed harmonising a new skill for the JP. I also wanted the PTR175 combined UHF and VHF radio. My experience of trying to establish low-level comms with the army on UHF line of sight only, convinced me we would have serious operating problems low-level over the jungle and we had to have VHF compatibility with the army ground radios.

Roger chose our target areas in Southern Malaysia, just across the Malacca Straits from Singapore. We had two Forward Air Control teams allocated to us which was not popular as FEAF were actually at war. The most experienced team was led by Captain Boulter who, when we started, was actually on board HMS Albion with his team. Typical Army compromise, the second team was from the Royal Corps of Transport, Lt. Peter Williams and his men. Unfortunately Pete had never heard of FAC and we had to teach him on the job. In the end he was more adaptable and better at the role in the jungle, probably because he did not come with previous training.

The teams took it in terms to set up about 6 targets a day for us out in the field and we all flew against them each day. We finally settled on homing on to a "Day-Glo" red meteorological balloon flying above the jungle canopy which indicated the position of the FAC. The FAC briefed the position of the target in bearing and distance from the balloon and gave a very detailed description of its location.

Now the targets had to be portable, easily set out and a challenge to find. We finally chose a 6 foot bivouac flysheet in jungle colours. Not only was it difficult for the aircrew to pick out but also very hard to identify on the gun camera film. However it worked well and we used it throughout the trial. The problem for the FAC was marking his own position, which was used as the IP, for the aircraft when he was under a 250 foot jungle canopy. The Met Office had self-inflating balloons which worked by initiating a carbide mixture to generate the gas. They could lift a 8 ½ ounce flare but in the end we decided we did not need that as given an accurate position on the map the balloon showed up well against the jungle canopy.

The techniques was to fly up to, and outbound from, the balloon at various heights and speeds. These were some of the parameters of the trial which Roger Noades needed to establish to recommend the best height and speed for the task. I think we tried 250ft above the canopy, 500 ft and 1,000 ft –some even higher at 3,000 feet. The runs were made at varying speeds from 120 kts, 180, 240 and even 300 knots – although that was pushing the poor old JP4 to the limit. Mind you I am not sure what the Hunter and the Canberra would have made of 120 kts!

We also had seconded to the unit Flt Lt Roger Austin from 20 Sqn, an absolute asset to the unit and he eventually went on to be a famous Air Marshal in his later career. One of the advantages of the JP, apart from being a very cheap trials aircraft was that having side-by-side seating it was possible to test for the advantages of having a second member of the crew to lookout for the target. For this role we had some Flying Officer second pilots from the FEAF Hastings transport force also added to the unit. This could be a miserable job. If the captain saw the target first, he pressed the recorder button and tried to get film of an attack as fast as he could. This usually involved a maximum G turn and pull-up for the dive.

Often the first thing the co-pilot knew was when he was blacked out and came round half-way down the slope – very sick making when you are not flying the aircraft. Of course if the co-pilot saw it first he would take control and turn on to the target. What Roger Noades wanted for his scientific study was not always convenient with what flying we wanted to do. However, it was absolutely clear that Roger called the shots. He set us a very ambitious target programme of initially 6 details a day, with two aircraft, 30 runs from each aircraft. The first phase of the trial was planned for over 2,000 target runs with a carefully calculated, statistically correct, combination of conditions.

One of my concerns was target fixation. It would have been all too easy in the enthusiasm to bring back a successfully filmed picture of the target against the clock to forget about pull out heights. In fact the only serious incident we had was not directly from that cause. One of our very experienced pilots had pulled out from an attack and was climbing away gently when he did not see a loan tree top sticking up above the jungle canopy but which was below the jungle skyline. He flew through the top of the tree and was very lucky to stay airborne. It said a lot for the strength of the JP that he could fly it back home.

XS224 after flying through a jungle tree. This picture was taken inside the inflatable Kidde Hangar at Tengah and shows the damage to the leading edge of the wings. (Mick Ryan)

One of the advantages of having put the JPs together ourselves was that we could repair the damage by replacing the wings, which were flown out from UK, with our own unit resources. Therefore it was strictly a Category 2 flying accident repaired from within unit resources and not a Cat 3, Major Accident, which it would have been under normal circumstances. I got criticised by "armchair warriors" in MOD later because I got the pilot flying again the next day. However, both he and I felt it was the right thing to do. Unfortunately the second trial which continued in 1966, with fresh personnel, but the same airframes, I understand had a fatality with a JP flying into the trees.

After the first six weeks we had exhausted the suitable target areas in Southern Malaysia, which anyway was semi-cultivated jungle terrain. So we moved everything up to the RAAF base at Butterworth three-quarters of the way up the left side of Malaysia on 11th October 1965. We operated from there for the rest of the year until the end of November 1965.

Here we were opposite the very rough jungle terrain covering the backbone of Central Malaysia. The professional FAC team actually deployed fulltime into the jungle by helicopter. They camped there in the Centre of Malaysia. It was dangerous country as the guerrillas continually came down from the Thai border and penetrated the jungle in that part of Malaysia trying to create trouble. Captain Boulter had his team on stand to before dawn every day to guard against guerrilla bands. He would then put out up to six flysheets in the edge of suitable clearings anything up to two or three miles round his central position noting features which he felt would help us locate them during his FAC talk-in.

The other team under Pete Williams drove out by Landrover from Butterworth every day and set up inside the jungle at different locations. His team also put out up to 6 flysheets – sometimes in more open partly cultivated jungle but this was realistic as air support was often required against intruders in this type of terrain as well. Although he returned to base every day, Pete penetrated into some very hairy jungle locations with his LandRovers. Unfortunately after the trial was over, Pete's LandRover rolled down a hill and he was badly injured.

During this time of the year in that part of the country the weather was not very suitable. We tried several combinations but ended up getting up very early and flying our sorties in the early part of the day before the clouds and thunderstorms built up inland.

We had one rather amusing incident which made us appreciate the performance of the JP4. HMS Ark Royal had an engine problem half way up the Straits of Malacca just opposite Penang Island. It was decided that she was too much of a target sitting there wallowing, unable to move, and that her aircraft should be flown off and landed at Butterworth. The night before Bob Innes in his inimitable "Yarpie" style said: "Presumably we're not flying tomorrow, Boss?" When asked to explain he said Naval pilots do not do landings they just flypast the carrier and are either hooked out of the sky or go round again until they connect. Round outs and touchdowns are unfamiliar to them.

I was not impressed and said we would fly as usual. When I returned to Butterworth from my first sortie the next morning at about 745, as usual I was low on fuel having come from the centre of the Malaysian peninsula. When I called joining I was told to stand off as they had one naval aircraft off the runway in the storm drain and another Sea Vixen had burst a tyre on landing and left debris all the way down the runway. I pointed out that I did not have enough fuel to hold off for long and asked where the Sea Vixen had first touched down. They said about 4 to 500 yards into the runway. I said I was going to have to land but only needed the first few hundred yards to stop a JP. I landed and turned off well before the debris. I apologised to Bob Innes and admitted that he had been right. We got the deck chairs out and watched the fun for the rest of the day.

The original plan had been to move the trial to Borneo to use the real terrain where the confrontation was taking place. However, the operators in Borneo did not want three trial aircraft interfering with their operations. So instead I was sent to Borneo to fly over the actual terrain and make sure the areas that we were using in Central Malaysian were representative of the war theatre.

When I landed at Kuching I was met off the aircraft by my old Wing Commander Flying at RAF Jever, Wing Commander Geoff Atherton, a very hard Australian who did not mince his words. As I stepped on to the concrete he shook my hand and said "Hello Mick, F--- off!" I got the message. I flew for a few days in Single and Twin Pioneers all over the border areas where there were insurgents. We had lost a few aircraft because the maps were blank and the border ill-defined. The C-in-C FEAF had just decreed that the next pilot to cross the border into Indonesia would be court martialled.

One of our Pioneer trips delivering goods and people to the border posts was following the L shaped border where Indonesia was inside the L. We set off from one short strip and headed off on 230 degrees. After a while an airfield appeared below with a "Thatched" Hercules transport just off the runway half way down. The pilots swore and dived back the way we had come telling me in an agitated voice that it was an Indonesian airfield heavily guarded by anti-aircraft guns and that the Hercules was there after we had shot it down - "Thatched" whilst they waited to repair it. Fortunately they must have been slightly more surprised than we were and no guns fired.

On landing we compared notes on the maps. All the squadron pilots had been issued with fablon covered maps with the regular routes marked on them permanently, giving heading and time. I pointed out that our route was mislabelled 230 degrees instead of the 270 degrees which was what was required to go round the inside of the L. I promised to say nothing as long as he had all the maps withdrawn from all squadron crews as they had all been made up by the Wing Navigation officer with the same mistake.

I was satisfied that the terrain in Central Malaysia was very representative of the Borneo area and that we did not need to deploy the 400 plus nautical miles to Kuching. I am sure that we would not have been allowed there anyway.

We had a lively time at Butterworth – I was arrested by the RAAF Military Police twice – once for stealing my own LandRover and once for taking a dip in the station swimming pool after a guest night – it all seemed like a good idea at the time!

We completed the number of runs that Roger required for his statistical analysis and apart from a few promotional flights for the Royal Malaysian Air Force in the hope that they would buy the BAC167 Strikemaster– we finished flying at the end of November. I managed 107 hours, 135 sorties, during the detachment, 64% were actual trial flights.

I never did see the final statistical conclusions of the trial. I was posted on return to the UK and only heard of the second phase some time afterwards. My impression was that about 240 knots, 500 feet and single seat was probably going to come out on top – but I stand to be corrected. We were very good at finding six foot bivouac flysheets – we would probably have flown right past a tank!

APPENDIX TWO
Leeming and the 'Paraffin Budgie'

No.3 Flying Training School was reformed at Leeming in September 1961 as a new Jet Provost training unit; the T.Mk.4 was also at the station throughout the 1960s. In December 1973 the Refresher Flying School moved to the station from Manby, and by 1977 it had become Refresher Flying Squadron. No.3 FTS was disbanded on 24 April 1984, when the station was closed whilst the site was prepared for the F3 Tornado. Interestingly, when the first Tornados appeared at the station for the locals to look at, they hardly ever thrashed around the circuit, taking a far more sedate approach. By contrast, twenty-odd JPs were far noisier! The author was stationed at Leeming between 1981-83; the following account describes the day to day experience of working on the line.

THE LINE

RAF Leeming operated over twenty Jet Provosts, T.Mk.3A & T.Mk.5A, during the late 70s and early 80s, flown by 3 FTS and RFS. Jet Provosts were not the only lodgers at the station. A number Bulldogs providing Elementary Flying Training for the Fleet Air Arm, a handful of Chipmunks flown by No.11 Air Experience Flying, and, on occasion, the original vintage pair also took the circuit. The Meteor and Vampire were Central Flying School's display team, until tragically both aircraft were lost in an incident on 25 May 1985 at Mildenhall; both crew on the Meteor perished. The station had a busy Visiting Aircraft Section (VAS) as the runway was one of the last remaining Major Diversion Airfields. When not flying, the serviceable were housed in 4 'shed' which opened directly onto the pan; incidentally, the doors displayed shrapnel scars from a wartime raid. The wartime hangar was cavernous and could easily cope with twenty aircraft at once. They were skilfully 'knitted' into four rows by two tug drivers, both civilian. In two years I only saw one collision in the hangar and then it was just a crack to a tip-tank light. The Bowser drivers on the line were also civilians, although they were ex-RAF.

The line shifts were a godsend. Whilst the majority the station worked from 8.00am until 5.00pm, if you were a 'liney' you worked 6.00am-12.30pm or 12.00 noon– 6.00pm. The morning/afternoon shift swapped each day, which meant each team had a long weekend every other week. In those days, opening hours at the pub was far more regulated than today, with most only open for tweo hours over lunch and not reopening until 7.00pm in the evening. However, when the market was in

The author in February 1983, the last day on Leeming Line.

town, things were radically different. Then the pubs were open until 4.00pm in the afternoon, closed for an hour (on occasion just to sweep out), and then off again! Naturally, every other afternoon we frequented a different market town and got to know Ripon, Thirsk, Northallerton and Bedale like the backs of our hands. There was the odd moment of culture: North Yorkshire contains many archaeological sites, and a group of us could often be found at Richmond and Helmsley Castle or Fountains, Byland and Riveaux Abbey – or at least in the pub near them.

The entire shift compliment went to breakfast in the mess around 5.30am. It has to be said that the breakfasts at Leeming were second to none. In nearly thirty years on military sites it has still never been beaten in my opinion. Especially the fried bread, it was so crispy it quite literally exploded when you stuck your knife into and there was a huge hotplate for frying eggs – being a Yorkshire man it was bliss! Hanging from the mess ceiling was a large model of a T.Mk.3A Jet Provost that, naturally, went missing from time to time. It had been returned from all over the UK – I remember it arriving back after a trip in a Shackleton to Lossimouth; the last I heard it had ended up at Conningsby after a Phantom detachment.

Once in a while, 'keys' came around. Two of the shift drew the keys from the guardroom and unlocked both the hangar and Handling Section. The duty also required the battery voltage and radio pressures to be checked on all aircraft; however, far more important was ensuring the tea urn was on! The late shift had two lineys to lock up once everyone else had cleared off.

On arrival at work, everyone was allocated three aircraft for Before Flight (BF) service. This had to be done before the aircraft were towed out for 8am; any unservicabilities were reported at this point – usually just blown bulbs in the cockpit. The F700s were laid out in the documents control office, run on our shift by a Sergeant and Chief Tech, and were signed up by the returning BF Liney. Whilst this was going on, other members of the team were taking out the CO_2 fire extinguishers, leaving one on every other slot. Meanwhile, the shift tractor driver towed out at least 10 Trolley Accumulators, again onto just about every other slot. The Jet Provost had two batteries but no auxiliary power unit (APU) or other means by which to run up the engine. Consequently, on the first start of the day the batteries needed a bit of help – basically a jumpstart – hence the Trolley Acc. After an hour's flying they were okay for the rest of the day. The Trolley Accs. were stored overnight on a charging point at Ground Electric. Only three were supposed be towed any one time; however, the temptation to tow four or more occasionally got the better of the driver, and unless you crawled along they snaked around like an overloaded caravan on the motorway. On more than one occasion the last one on an exceptionally long train would turn over – major inquiry all-round. By 8 o'clock the line was full of Jet Provosts waiting in quiet anticipation for the day's flying.

A number of specific activities were performed throughout the day to keep the aircraft operational and the line running smoothly. The busiest and probably most pivotal roles was that of the marshaller. It was his job to park the aircraft on the required slot as they taxied back in from their first and subsequent sorties. He was in constant communication with two Line Controllers, who, in turn, were in contact with Air Traffic Control. The line controllers at Leeming were two extremely ancient Navigator Warrant Officers. Nobody actually knew how old they were, but Lancasters were mentioned on more than one occasion. They lived in a small watchtower-type of extension to Handling Flight, supplied with a radio, telephone and map of the line on which they moved small cut-out Jet Provosts. As the aircraft touched down, ATC informed the Controllers who, in turn, radioed the parking slot to the marshaller. Once the first wave was airborne, the marshaller didn't have much time sit down!

The refuel team comprised two of the shift who, as the name suggests, refuelled the aircraft after each flight and at the end of the day. The aircraft were always hangared full, so the pace only quickened once the first wave was landing back at the station. The Jet Provost was old school when it came to refuelling, as it was open line – so similar to filling the car at a garage. The tanks were pressurised by ram air that sometimes remained after engine shut down. It was not unusual for the fuel cap, especially on the T.Mk.3A tip tank, to achieve a few feet in the air if you were skilled at flicking open the lid! Open line also had its hazards. Again on the T.Mk.3A the process was to fill the wing tanks and then the tips; occasionally, if most of the fuel had been used and the landing light especially on a solo trip, the main oleo would stay high. Once the weight of fuel started to build, the oleo would drop, forcing fuel to rush up the tank and squirt back out of the filling point, down the wing and all over the pan. In cases like that the controllers called for a pan wash, as the fuel had a detrimental effect on the aircraft tyres; the fire service dispatched a tender onto the line and promptly washed the spill down the nearest storm drain! The T.Mk.5A presented its own unique hazard. The last few feet of the wing leading edge was modified by painting a very aggressive type of artex on it. This was part of the anti-oscillation measures incorporated after the discovery that the type was dangerous in a spin. The problem was it was very easy to leave several layers of skin on it, as it lay close to the refuel point.

Once the aircraft had flown and returned, it required a turn-a-round; a check for damage, replenishment of engine oils and oxygen if required, along with the seat straps being sorted out. Each shift ran two teams, who descended on the aircraft once the marshaller had parked the JP up. The teams were supervised by a Corporal who walked the line over, signing the F705 flight servicing sheet and checking any suspected snag. This was also the point at which the refuelling team turned up. Surprisingly, very little tended to show up from one flight to the next. One problem did beset both types operated at Leeming – cracks in the jet pipe shroud. On discovering the crack, the walker radioed the snag into the line controllers. They then telephoned through to the rectification flight, who dispatched a fitter, usually chap called Taff Thomas, by bicycle, armed with a hand drill and 1/8th bit to stop drill the offending crack. Taff was a slightly wild-looking individual, especially hurtling along at full pelt on a workshop bicycle, complaining bitterly that his game of 'ukkers' had been disturbed yet again. He held the dubious honour of being able to down eight pints of Theakston's Old Peculiar snakebites in the Buffs Lodge, leaving most of us struggling on our second or third! Cracks continued to be stop drilled until the aircraft was taken off the line for deeper servicing or the crack was 'beyond limits'; then it was welded up by workshops. If the aircraft was low on oxygen, the nose compartment was left open by the turn-a-round team as a signal to the duty 'gasman'. A second driver, usually Ian Paterson or John Roberts, towed out a set of bottles and charged the system backup. I remember, one day, the charging hose split at the regulator end of the trolley with an extremely loud bang. Ian cleared the bottle set with one leap so he could get to the key and close it off. 3000psi escaping from a small hole caused a lot of static and, by turning off the bottle, a very serious situation had been averted.

The rest of the shift were put on the 'see-offs'. Aircrew would appear in the 700 office, check the log and then sign to accept the aircraft. Meanwhile, the phone would go on the line controller's desk requesting a start-up crew for a particular aircraft. The T.Mk.3As were all designated letters phonetically (e.g. Juliet, November, Romeo), whilst the T.Mk.5As ran from the early 50s to late 60s in number. The entire see-off teams' names were on map pins on the controller's desk; the one at the top went out and waited for the crew. The first job on reaching the aircraft was to remove one set of chocks from the main wheel, put them in the nose, and then remove the other main set completely. Not always as easy as you would think, especially if the refuel crew didn't spread the chocks from the wheel a few inches before filling up. When the aircraft settled under the additional fuel, the chocks would get pinched by the tyres. Sometimes you had to bash chocks out with the aid of another one; naturally, this did not fill a new student with confidence as he walked out. After checking the surfaces and structure the crew climbed in. Once in the cockpit, the groundcrew aided the strap in passing the top straps and leg restraints, and then, on the say-so of the pilot, removed the top ejection seat pins. This was carried out in a set order: canopy jettison first, furthest face screen then nearest. The last thing you wanted to do was to lean over a live ejection seat with a nervous student wobbling about in it trying to find the handle for the height adjuster!

Eventually the crew were ready to start the engine; the customary one finger spin was signalled from the cockpit and after a quick look around the groundcrew did the same. The engine whined into life – but not always. Occasionally the engine flooded.

'If RPM stabilize at 15% (wet start)
Set HP cock CLOSED. Ignition switch OFF. Drain collector tanks and jet pipe. Carry out dry run. Close collector tank and jet pipe drains. Repeat start using a different power supply.'

AP 101B-2305-14C. Jet Provost T.Mk.5A Normal Drills.

Sounds easy! Well it was for the aircrew. Whoever was doing the see-off had to crawl under the aircraft and remove the two drain plugs; problem was, with a full fuel load and two crew there wasn't much space between your face and the oily bottom of the aircraft. The dry run blew the excess fuel from the engine collector tank onto the pan, which naturally you ended up lying in whilst refitting the drain plugs. The aircraft usually ran up after that, often with an added bonus – fuel was routinely blown through the turbine and into the jet pipe rather than out through the drain. By the time the engine was reaching full temperature this had ignited giving, on occasion, a very satisfying flame or, if you were extremely lucky, ball of burning fuel.

Once the aircraft was running, the crew went through a number of control surface checks, including the flaps and spoilers with corresponding signals from the groundcrew. Once done, the pilot gave the 'thumbs up' then, after applying the parking brake, gave the chocks-out signal. It was at that point that you could leave skin on the T.Mk.5As nose strakes if you were not too careful. With chocks out and a flash of the landing lamps – on the T.Mk.3A so dim you could not see it in bright sunshine – the aircraft powered up and taxied out under the guidance of the groundcrew. With experienced aircrew, a see-off from start to finish took about fifteen minutes; if it was a student's first time or first solo this could extend to an hour – nice in summer, murder in February.

Each aircraft could fly up to four times a day, with the busiest time invariably during mid-day shift changeover. By five o'clock the majority of aircraft were back on the ground, and the afternoon turn-a-round teams converted to after-flight servicing, as did the see-off team. Once the aircraft were signed up they were towed back to the hangar, fully fuelled and ready for the following day.

A number of incidents spring to mind. During the summer of 1982, a large part of the United Kingdom was blighted with clouds of Green Fly. A number of aircraft were landed on 'Emergency State 2', using just instruments because they had flown at low-level through a cloud. The sheer amount of insects squashed up the windscreen blocked out all forward vision, forcing the QFI to call a potential emergency. Incidentally, anyone who has cleaned an aircraft windscreen in summer will know that insects clearly have 'araldite' for blood. The only way to remove them is by soaking them with hot water for a good ten minutes!

XW415 T.Mk5A based at Leeming but on charge with CFS (note crest on intake)

Cranwell 2008 XW353 T.Mk.5A. The author did 45 minutes in this aircraft 25 years ago!

After an exceptionally well placed Christmas and New Year over 1981-1982, the aircraft had been parked up in the hangar for nearly two weeks. Naturally, they were all BF'd before being towed onto the line. As the aircraft reached the allotted slot, the chap on brakes was signalled by the towing chief to put on the brakes. This was achieved on the JP by depressing the toe peddles on the rudder bar. The chief then unhitched the tractor and put in a set of chocks; the brakes were then released and the aircraft left. Unfortunately, this application of brakes did not necessarily demonstrate the integrity of the brake system. The Jet Provost relies on a process of differential braking, with the nose leg castoring left or right to manoeuvre whilst on the ground. I remember quite distinctly having to leap out of the way as the aircraft I was marshalling apparently ignored my signal to turn right and ran straight for me onto the grass. Once a few more ended up off the concrete, all flying was suspended until the entire fleet at Leeming, and I suspect elsewhere, had had their brakes checked out.

Flying was another plus in working with the training fleet. The majority of the line had flown quite a few hours over the years, and there is still something exhilarating about recalling those flights twenty-five years later. My parents lived near Scarborough in a village only about thirty minutes' flying time from Leeming, and it became quite a regular thing to buzz the house. The general route entailed flying east out of circuit over the Moors, with Fylingdales in the distance, to Whitby. Then down the coast to Scarborough, around the castle headland at about 1,000ft, and then dropping down to around 200ft for a run westerly inland to Pickering. The Vale of Pickering was a low-flying zone, with Staxton Wold radar station on the Wold scarp and CSOS Irton Moor on the opposing hillside. Seamer, and, on occasion, my dad sleeping after a night shift, was slap in the middle. I used to phone up and describe what was on the washing line! For a good year after I was posted to Lyneham, a number of pilots used to 'bounce' the house. Another heart-stopper was the tail chase and low-level in the Lakes. The old adage went: 'If you can't see the cows legs you're too high, but if you can see the sheep's legs you're too low'. I've certainly been low enough to wave up to walkers before now!

Not everyone found it such fun, I'm sure. Once, when I was line marshaller, a request crackled through on the radio to park Romeo, a T.Mk.3A, on the furthest slot on the line from the Handling Flight. As it was already coming up the pan, I hitched a lift on the tractor, using some colourful language as we drove past a good fifteen slots that were empty. It was only after the aircraft shut down that we realised why we were so far away from anything. The student had wet himself, and, as punishment for not preparing for the hour-long flight, the QFI made him walk the entire length of the pan with a wet backside. He jokingly threatened the tractor driver with a charge if he offered the dejected young man a lift! And it wasn't just the aircrew that had such 'accidents'. Once, on a three ship tail chase, the third aircraft had to return prematurely to base. On landing, it became apparent that there had been a bit of an 'accident' in the cockpit. The groundcrew member who had been in the spare seat had been unable to keep hold of his lunch; unfortunately, he had his oxygen mask on at the time. He promptly filled the mask, assisted by a negative-g manoeuvre, and the liquid migrated back into his helmet; the stink was unimaginable.

Poachers Commentary 1976

Good afternoon ladies and gentlemen. I am Flying Officer Ken Claxton, the adjutant of the Poachers' Formation aerobatic team, which is next on your programme. On behalf of the team I would like to say how pleased we are to be here at — today.

The Poachers team is based at Cranwell in Lincolnshire. The members of the team are all flying instructors at the Royal Air Force College and therefore have to practice their aerobatic manoeuvres mainly in their spare time. This is generally early in the morning or late afternoon, before and after instructional flying.

Today's weather conditions should allow a — display, and during the display I shall be telling you a little about the pilots, the aircraft, and the formation changes as they occur.

The display lasts for about twelve minutes and this year's new additions are the upward split, followed by two pairs of aircraft passing head-on, and also one of the most difficult manoeuvres of the display, – the Line Astern Loop, (the display finishes with the new French Break to land).

If you look to your front you will see the team approaching at about 300mph and 500ft above the ground in wide box. Their first manoeuvre is a Box join up loop, in which they aim to be in close formation at the top of the loop. Box is the basic formation and many formation changes involve going through Box at some stage.

The leader, who is now out in front of the formation, is Sqn Ldr Peter Curtin, now in his second years as leader. You can now see him positioning the aircraft for a barrel roll, which will be completed in the team's famous Swan formation. Swan is the formation depicted on the Poachers' badge.

Peter, from Worthing Sussex, was born at Tunbridge wells and was educated at Ardingly College, where he was a member of the Combined Cadet Force. He joined the RAF as a Flight Cadet at Cranwell in 1955, and now has 5,000 flying hours to his credit, mainly on Hunters and Canberras. Peter is married and presently commands a squadron at Cranwell.

You can now see Peter calling the formation back into box before going to Tee formation. As you see, the aircraft form the shape of a letter 'T' with the Nos 2 and 3 flying line abreast of the leader and No. 4 flying astern.

The aircraft closest to you is the No. 2, flown by Flt Lt Philip Boreham. Philip, whose parents now live in Bournemouth, is in his first year with the team. He was born in India and educated in the West Indies. His last three years at school were spent at Shaftesbury Grammar School in Dorset. Philip joined the RAF in 1964 and has

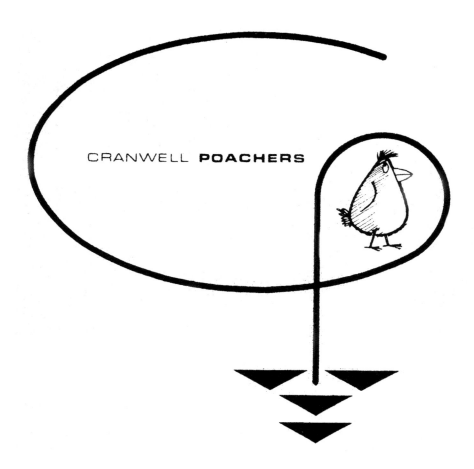

Poachers' Logo (with addition!)

2,600 hours, flying Canberras in Germany and Phantoms with 54 Sqn. He is married and now lives in Leasingham, Lincs.

The team now goes into Echelon starboard to prepare for the twizzle and join up.

This year the team is flying the Jet Provost Mk.5A. The A signifies that it's a basic Jet Provost Mk.5 but with improved navigational equipment. It is used at the RAF College for the basic flying training of student pilots. It is powered by a Bristol Siddeley Viper engine with a thrust of 2,500lb, has a maximum speed of about 400mph, and is capable of flying at heights up to 38,000ft.

Next comes the line astern loop.

The team again goes through Box to change into Swan formation for a Swan clover.

The leader is now calling the aircraft into Card, in which the aircraft form a square. When pointing vertically upwards, the formation will split into two pairs and then close head-on at 600mph.

The pair on your — is being led by Fly Lt Stoner, who is the No. 3 and also the team's deputy leader. He is married and has a son and lives in Navenby Lincs. He was educated at Buckland School in Devon and Joined the RAF as a Cranwell Flight Cadet

XW357 T.Mk.5 of the Cranwell Poachers in 1976.

in 1966. Martin was last flying Lightning Fighters with No. 19 Squadron in Germany, and is now in his second year with the Poachers.

If you've noticed Martin's unsteadiness in the formation so far, its probably because he's thinking about next year. He joins the Red Arrows this coming October for three years.

The team has now joined up in Line Astern and Sqd Ldr Peter Curtin is calling them into Box midway through a Barrel Roll.

You can now see the No. 4 drop down to the bottom of the formation to form what the team call Finger 4.

This year's No. 4 is Flt Lt David Webley of Sutton Coalfield who is, again, in his second year in the team. He attended Oundle School and gained an Honours Degree in Engineering at Loughborough College of Advanced Technology.

The No. 2 is now taking up a Line Abreast position on the leader to form Rhombus formation, for the completion of a loop.

David, who is married, with two daughters, started his flying career with Nottingham University Air Squadron, joined the RAF in 1966 and, like Martin, flew Lightnings with No. 19 Sqn in Germany.

The team now changes to Wine Glass with the leader on the — the No. 2 on the — and Nos 3 and 4 in Line Astern.

Reforming in Box the team now enters its final looping manoeuvre, before descending again to 500ft and a Cascade Split. The aircraft now reform as quickly as possible.

Ladies and gentlemen, thank you for your attention during the past ten minutes, and I hope that you have enjoyed the Poachers' Display.

Bibliography

BOOKS

Clarke, B., 2005, *Four Minute Warning; Britain's Cold War* (Tempus Publishing, Stroud)

Gardner, C., 1981, *British Aircraft Corporation; A History* BT (Batsford Ltd, London)

Healey,D., 1989, *The Time of my Life* (Penguin Books)

Johnson, B., 1986, *Test Pilot* (BBC Publications)

Macmillan, H., 1971, *Riding the Storm 1956-1959* (Macmillan, London)

Saunders, H.St.G., 1944, *Per Ardua: The Rise of British Airpower 1911 – 1939* (Oxford University Press, London)

Simmons, G. & Abraham, B., 2001, *Strong Foundations: Driffield's Aerodrome from 1917 to 2000* (Hutton Press Ltd, Beverley)

Sturtivant,R., Hamlin, J., & Halley, J.J., 1997, *Royal Air Force Flying Training and Support Units* (Air-Britain Publications)

Wilson, H., 1971, *The Labour Government 1964-1970: A Personal Record* (Weindenfeld/Michael Joseph)

Ziegler, P., 1985, *Mountbatten: the Official Biography* (Book Club Associates)

GOVERNMENT DOCUMENTS

7 March 1957, Secretary of State for Air, George Ward, Vote A. Number for Air Force Service. Commons Sitting. Hansard.

AAIB Bulletin No. 8/2003. Ref. EW/C2002/08/04.

AAIB Bulletin No: Ref:EW/G2001/02/06.

Accident to Jet Provost XD680 on 1-9-55, Accidents Investigation Branch, 15 November 1956 (PRO (AVIA 5/34)).

Aircraft Accident Involving Royal Air Force Jet Provost T3 XN590. Military Aircraft Accident Summaries MAAS 5/82 19 February 1982.

Aircraft Accident Involving Royal Air Force Jet Provost T3A XN641. Military Aircraft Accident Summaries MAAS 6/85/2 24 April 1985.

Aircraft Accident Involving Royal Air Force Jet Provost T3A XN643. Military Aircraft Accident Summaries MAAS 2/83 8 February 1983.

Aircraft Accident Involving Royal Air Force Jet Provost T5A XW288. Military Aircraft Accident Summaries MAAS 20/83 12 July 1983.

Aircraft Accident Involving Royal Air Force Jet Provost T5A XW407 & XW411. Military Aircraft Accident Summaries MAAS 1/87 9 February 1987.

Aircraft Accident Involving Royal Air Force Jet Provost T5A XW417. Military Aircraft Accident Summaries MAAS 13/84 4 April 1984.

Aircraft Accident involving the Royal Air Force Jet Provost T3A XN473. Military aircraft accident summaries: MAAS 9/85. 14 May 1985.

Aircraft Accident involving the Royal Air Force Jet Provost T3A XM453. Military aircraft accident summaries: MAAS 17/84. 26 September 1984.

Aircraft Accident involving the Royal Air Force Jet Provost T5A XW308. Military aircraft accident summaries: MAAS 3/82. 10 February 1982.

Aircraft and Engine Performance Tests on a Jet Provost fitted with a Viper 11 Engine Bristol Siddeley Engines. Report No.V.11/1. June 1959.

Electromagnetic Compatibility of Weapons Fitted to BAC-167 Strikemaster MK 87 Aircraft. MAS Ref: AV/583/029. 20th January 1970.

Fatigue Loadings in Flight. Tech Note No. Structures 260. February 1959.

First Prototype Jet Provost T.Mk.5 XS230. Despatch Brochure for A&AEE Boscombe Down. Flight Test Report AFN/JP/8.

Full Scale Spinning Tests on the Percival Provost Mk.1. Ministry of Supply.

Jet Provost MK 5 – Miniature Detonating Cord Clearance Trials. MOD Ref AH/563/02 24 May 1973.

Jet Provost MKS 3 and 4 - Ejection Through Canopy Trials. MOD Ref AH/661/047 13 November 1974.

Jet Provost Prototype T.Mk.3 G-23-1. Qualitative Preview Handling Assessment. AAEE/875/3 April 1958 (AVIA 18/4244).

Jet Provost T.Mk.2 – Cockpit Layout Ref. QF 210.

Ministry of Supply AirB2(a), Jet Provost Mark 3, 29 January 1957. (PRO T 225/810).

Ministry of Supply DM.233/645/025, Jet Provost T.Mk.3, 19 January 1959. (PRO T 225/810).

Ministry of Supply, Jet Provost Mark III, 22 February 1959. (PRO T 225/810).

Poachers Commentary 1976, Central Flying School. RAFC Cranwell.

Report on the 150 hour Development Flight Testing of Viper 8 Engine V.1505 in Hunting Mk.II Jet Provost XD.694 (April 1958).

Security Council resolution 82 (1950) Resolution of 25 June 1950.

Standard Operating Procedures The Poachers 1976.

Tech Note Aero.2366. August 1955.

The Poachers 1975. Training Command Flight Safety Magazine. Jan-Mar 1976.

Air Publications

AP 101B-230¾/5-5A2: Jet Provost Safety And Servicing Notes.

AP 101B-2303 & 4-15: Pilots Notes Jet Provost T Mk 4.

AP 101B-2303A-15: Jet Provost T Mk 3A Aircrew Manual.

AP 101B-2305-15 Jet Provost T Mk 5A Aircrew Manual with T Mk 5 Supplement.

AP 4349A Provost T1 Pilots Notes.

AP 4254A Prentice 1 Pilots Notes.

OTHER SOURCES

Australian Transport Safety Bureau Ref. Nov2007/DOTARS 50390.

Court Of Magistrates (Malta) As A Court Of Criminal Judicature. Magistrate Dr. Antonio Micallef Trigona. Sitting of the 10th January, 2008. Number 479/2007.

The Observer, Sunday June 29 2003. Antony Barnett, Public Affairs Editor.

Finally the excellent web-based research project by Mark Russell
http://www.jetprovostheaven.co